A FIRST CHURCH HISTORY

A FIRST
CHURCH HISTORY

WITH AN ILLUSTRATED TIME-CHART
AND A SHORT BOOK-LIST FOR
STUDENTS AND TEACHERS

VERA E. WALKER

SCM PRESS LTD
BLOOMSBURY STREET LONDON

First published March 1936
Second impression November 1939
Third impression May 1943
Fourth impression November 1944
Fifth impression September 1946
Sixth impression December 1948
Seventh impression January 1951
Eighth impression January 1954
Ninth impression September 1956
Tenth impression April 1961

PRINTED IN GREAT BRITAIN

PREFACE

THIS is a first simple history of the Christian Church, intended for all persons over twelve years of age. It is not a history of the Church in this country, though, as it is written mainly for English readers, it is natural that the British Isles should have a large part in it. It is some account of the Church in all the centuries and in all countries, and its main biographies include those of three Frenchmen, three Italians, a German, a Spaniard, an African, a Belgian, and a Dutchman.

It is also a history of the Christian Churches; of all that call themselves by that name, even though they deny that right to some of their neighbours. It tries to tell the story of each group of Christians fairly and sympathetically, not in order to perpetuate " our unhappy divisions," but in the belief that they can be reconciled only when they are properly understood.

If this book strengthens the reader's loyalty to his own Church and deepens his understanding of that of other Christians, it will do something to prepare the way for the reunion of Christendom.

" Holy Church am I," quoth she,
" Thou oughtest me to know."
                    PIERS PLOWMAN

CONTENTS

PREFACE v

I. THE FIRST CHRISTIANS 1
First and Second Centuries

II. THE WITNESS OF THE MARTYRS 12
Second and Third Centuries

III. THE WAR AGAINST WORLDLINESS 20
Fourth Century

IV. THE BATTLE FOR THE FAITH 27
Fourth Century

V. THE GOVERNMENT AND DISCIPLINE OF THE CHURCH 35
Fourth and Fifth Centuries

VI. THE SERVICE OF GOD 44
Fifth and Sixth Centuries

VII. THE MISSIONARIES TO THE WEST 51
Fifth to Eighth Centuries

VIII. A CHRISTIAN EMPIRE IN EUROPE 59
Ninth and Tenth Centuries

IX. THE CHURCH IN THE BYZANTINE EMPIRE 67
Ninth to Eleventh Centuries

X. TEMPORAL AND SPIRITUAL POWER 75
Twelfth Century

XI. THE FRIARS   84
    Thirteenth Century

XII. THE WITNESS OF NOBLE MEN   93
    Thirteenth Century

XIII. THE ORGANISATION OF LEARNING   101
    Thirteenth Century

XIV. THE WORSHIP OF THE MIDDLE AGES   108
    Thirteenth and Fourteenth Centuries

XV. THE NEW LEARNING   117
    Fifteenth and Sixteenth Centuries

XVI. THE PROTESTANTS   127
    Sixteenth Century

XVII. THE REFORMED CHURCH   137
    Sixteenth Century

XVIII. THE ROMAN CATHOLICS   145
    Sixteenth Century

XIX. THE CHURCH OF ENGLAND   152
    Sixteenth Century

XX. THE FREE CHURCHES   161
    Seventeenth Century

XXI. THE SOCIETY OF FRIENDS   172
    Seventeenth Century

XXII. THE CHURCH OF SCOTLAND   179
    Seventeenth Century

XXIII. CHRISTIAN CHARITY   187
    Seventeenth Century

XXIV. THE EVANGELICAL REVIVAL   194
    Eighteenth Century

XXV. THE ANGLO-CATHOLIC REVIVAL   203
Nineteenth Century

XXVI. THE WORLD FOR CHRIST   214
Nineteenth Century

XXVII. CHRISTIAN FELLOWSHIP   225
Nineteenth Century

XXVIII. THE SALVATION ARMY   231
Nineteenth and Twentieth Centuries

XXIX. " THE NATIONS SHALL BRING THEIR GLORY "   238
Nineteenth and Twentieth Centuries

XXX. CHRIST OR CÆSAR ?   246
Nineteenth and Twentieth Centuries

XXXI. THAT THEY MAY BE ONE   257
Nineteenth and Twentieth Centuries

EPILOGUE   263

A SHORT BOOK–LIST   265

INDEX   273

TIME CHART   At End
Designed by May Ollis Pelton
Illustrated by Doris Pailthorpe

CHAPTER I
THE FIRST CHRISTIANS
First and Second Centuries

The Roman Empire in the first century after Christ was a deep belt of land all round the Mediterranean Sea. The north of Britain was its most northerly point, Spain its most westerly, Chaldea marked its farthest eastern limit, and to the south it went down into Egypt beyond Thebes. There were about a hundred million people living in it, mostly in the great cities, and the cultivated lands that surrounded them.

Those famous cities, with their majestic buildings, their temples, libraries, baths, gymnasia, schools, shops, markets and banks; the splendid smooth-paved roads which made a network covering the whole Empire; the great ships with their heavy freights of corn and their hundreds of passengers, were significant of the wealth and culture of the times. Round the Empire, "from Britain to Jerusalem and from Jerusalem to Morocco," the Roman legions threw their line or defence against the barbarians outside.

The people of the Empire were of many races

and many tongues, though west of Sicily Latin was the official language. They were conquered people, but, on the whole, they lived happily under the Roman rule. They were allowed their own customs, each country its national religion, and during the early part of this period they took a fair share of the government of their own cities. Only one thing was firmly insisted upon—the supremacy of the Emperor. Any gods could be worshipped—by Cæsar's consent; but Cæsar himself was above the gods, and a man's first loyalty was to the Empire.

In that great and splendid Empire, where so much was good, there was also much that was evil. The slave system was everywhere; and though some of the Emperors had made laws to prevent a slave being killed or tortured for no reason at all, yet the life of a slave could be a wretched one. He had practically no rights, he could be terribly ill-treated, and no redress was possible. Moreover, such power over fellow human beings has a dreadful effect on the character of those who use it, and the slave-owners were often worse men and women than their slaves. It was a cruel age. Parents literally threw away their unwanted babies; old people, who had neither relatives nor societies to care for them, perished miserably. Cruelty was fed and increased by the dreadful sights at the gladiatorial shows, where men and beasts dying in agony were exhibited as part of the afternoon's entertainment. There was an uncleanness in the life of the people, too bad to be described here.

There was one race in the Empire whose dogged fight for its particular faith and way of living had earned it special liberties—the race of the Jews. The Jews would neither recognise the existence of the gods of the heathen nor treat the Emperor as a god. They kept their own customs ; they had strict rules for living a pure life ; and though they owned slaves they never treated them as other races did, for a Jewish slave kept the Passover with his master, and therefore he too must be treated as one of the People of God.

It was from among these people that the Christian Church arose, a Church at one with the Jews in worship of the One True God, whose worship demands a life of kindness and purity. But the Christians differed from the Jews, and these differences aroused Jewish opposition. The Christians held that God had sent His Son, the Messiah, to reveal Himself to mankind and save them, and His Holy Spirit to help His followers to live the life He commanded them, and to spread the Faith among the nations. They invited any and all to join them, without first becoming Jews ; and their kindness went beyond that of the Jews, it overflowed to all around them.

The Christian Faith spread rapidly. St Paul carried it west, through Asia Minor, to Greece and Rome, and perhaps beyond. Persecution by the Jews scattered the Christians of Palestine, and when the Imperial armies besieged and took Jerusalem as a punishment for the Jewish political plots, they were dispersed further still. We have only old, dim, confused tales to tell us the names of the places to which the Apostles and Evangelists went, but old tales always have some truth in them, and if the Apostles themselves did not reach these places, their first disciples must have done so. Legends tell us that St Matthew went to Arabia, St Mark to Alexandria, St James to Spain, the family of Lazarus to Gaul, St Joseph of Arimathea to Glastonbury in England, St Thomas to India, St Jude to Syria and Persia, the others to Scythia, Mesopotamia, Asia, Chaldea. The tale which tells how St Andrew braved and converted the fierce Scythians was rewritten for us by an Anglo-Saxon poet in the eighth century, and is a fine bit of seafaring adventure which our ancestors must have loved to read.[1]

It is not easy to write a description of the first Christians; but from the very earliest Christian writings we possess we get an impression of people who were brimming over with a new joy, thrilled by a new idea, strong with a new life, and

[1] Cynewulf's *Andreas*.

yet wonderfully steady and serene. With all their faults—and they were not at all perfect people—there was a sore of radiance about them which healed and helped all those whom they met. One of the very earliest hymns ever sung in the Christian Church describes the Faith as a mighty river spreading life and healing wherever it goes. "For there went forth a stream and became a river, great and broad . . . the restrainers of the children of men were not able to restrain it . . . for it spread over the face of the whole earth and filled everything. Blessed are the ministers of that draught who are entrusted with that water of His : they have assuaged the dry lips and the will that had fainted they have raised up; and souls that were near departing they have caught back from death; and limbs that had fallen they have straightened and set up. They gave strength for their feebleness and light to their eyes : for everyone knew them in the Lord ; and they lived by the water of life for ever. Hallelujah." [1]

NOTES . . . .

CHRISTIAN LIFE.—At first the Christians, in Jerusalem at any rate, pooled their wealth and shared it as everyone had need; later, each kept his own, but no one was counted worthy of the

An Early Christian Psalter. Rendel Harris.

Name who would not help his poorer neighbour. They made collections for fellow-Christians in distress in other parts of the Empire, offered hospitality to travelling Apostles, and provided for such as had to give up their work on joining the Church. As Jews, the first Christians had been brought up to respect work of all kinds, and their Master had been a carpenter, so they worked at any trade which did not encourage wrong ways of thinking and living. But some trades and professions were impossible ; no Christian could be an idol-maker, or do anything connected with heathen worship, or be a gladiator. They hated the horrible entertainments where men and beasts were killed in the arena as part of an afternoon's entertainment. Though they were ready to suffer for their faith, they were especially anxious to relieve other people's sufferings wherever they found a chance to do so. Wealthy Christians sometimes collected sick people in their own homes, others devoted themselves especially to the service of the sick poor ; and when the great plagues swept through the cities, there are records of how Christians stayed to nurse and care for men and women of all creeds and classes.

BAPTISM.—Everyone who became a Christian was baptised, dipped under [1] running water in some stream or river, or, when that was impossible,

---

[1] This is called Immersion.

water was poured on his head in the Name of the Father and the Son and of the Holy Ghost; after that followed the laying-on of hands that the newly baptised might receive the Holy Spirit. It very soon became the custom to recite a short statement of belief before entering the water. These statements were the first CREEDS (Credo = I believe).

Baptism was such a solemn and important act that those learning to be Christians (catechumens) sometimes put it off as late as possible, being afraid of professing themselves of the Faith and then failing to live up to its standards. This was a bad custom. On the other hand, in quite early times we find that the children of Christian people were brought to be baptised, those who were responsible for them saying the Creed in their stead and promising to bring them up as Christians.

No grown person was baptised until he had been taught the Faith. At first this was done by any ordinary member of the Church. The Apostles taught by preaching, and by their letters. The first Life of Jesus had been written by A.D. 60, and the others by the end of the first century. Later there grew up a much longer and more elaborate system of education, and catechumens often had to wait some years before they were admitted to the Church. In the second century

Christians, at their baptism, publicly renounced the devil and all his pomps (the bad old heathen ways), were signed with the Cross and anointed with holy oil, and received Holy Communion immediately afterwards. Baptism generally took place on Easter Eve, and in the third century it became the custom to give those who were baptised a white robe as the symbol of their new life. If anyone who desired baptism died before he could receive it, or if any unbaptised Christian was martyred for his faith, the desire and the martyrdom counted for true baptism.

THE GOVERNMENT OF THE CHURCH.—The New Testament tells us of evangelists, ELDERS or PRESBYTERS, and DEACONS, who governed the Church under the leadership of the Apostles. Later, as we shall see, the highest officers in the Church were called BISHOPS (=overseers).

CHRISTIAN WORSHIP. — Christians began by worshipping in the Temple and the Synagogues, but it soon became necessary for them to have their own churches. They met at first in private houses ; when more room was needed they hired public buildings ; and later still they built their own churches in the style of an ordinary Roman court-house. These were plain rectangular buildings, with a semi-circular piece called an APSE jutting out at one of the short ends, and a porch at the other. In the apse, on a raised platform facing the congregation, and behind the ALTAR, sat the elders and whoever presided over the service, and between them and the congregation there was a rail or light lattice screen.

From St Paul's writings we know that in the Church services there were prayers, prophesyings, explanations of the prophecies, plain teaching, hymns, and readings from Scriptures and Apostolic letters. Men and women prayed or prophesied or sang hymns, sometimes alone, sometimes together, as in an Evangelical prayer-meeting. These meetings sometimes became disorderly, and in time a more formal worship began to take place, conducted by especially appointed persons.

The Lord's Supper was celebrated from Apostolic times, at first in the evening after a friendly meal called the *Agape*, or Love-feast. Later it was always celebrated in the very early morning, for when the persecutions began, the Christians were a hunted people who had to conceal what they did and admit only those of their own Faith. It came to be called by the beautiful name *Eucharist*, which means Thanksgiving, because joy and thanksgiving were the subject of its prayer and praise. We have records of some of those prayers written as early as A.D. 100, and in A.D. 150 JUSTIN MARTYR (see p. 18) gives us a rough outline of the service as it was in his own times. He tells first of the readings of Scriptures and letters from

Bishops ; of prayers for everyone ; of the giving
of the Kiss of Peace ; of the bringing up of
the Bread and Wine and Water (which had
been selected from other offerings which the
congregation had brought) ; of the great Prayer
of Thanksgiving and Consecration to which all
answered Amen ; of the Communion of the
people and the carrying away of the Consecrated
Bread to the sick and those who could not be
present at the service ; lastly, of the collection
that was made for the poor. A century after this
we find that those who officiated wore white
robes.

Though the order of the service was much the
same everywhere, beautiful and memorable words
and actions were naturally copied and repeated,
and in time various places—Rome, Alexandria,
Gaul and the Eastern Churches—each came to
have their own especial form of the service, or
LITURGY.

In the days of the persecutions the tombs of
the martyrs in the catacombs[1] were often used
as the Holy Table or Altar, and because of this
it became the custom afterwards to enclose the
relics of a martyr in the altar of a church.

The Eucharist was celebrated on special feast-
days. Sunday, being the day of the Resurrection,
was a festival, and there were others. First

---

[1] See p. 14.

Easter, then Pentecost, then Epiphany, then Christmas, began to be kept as yearly festivals. Christians prepared themselves for these days of solemn rejoicing by fasting as an act of reverence and discipline. They fasted for part of each day during the forty days before Easter (Lent), and till three o'clock every Wednesday and Friday, and before receiving Holy Communion.

When the persecutions began, the days on which the martyrs died were called their "Birthdays," because it was on that day that they entered the heavenly life, and these days came to be kept as Saints' days, or holy days.

CHAPTER II
THE WITNESS OF THE MARTYRS
SECOND AND THIRD CENTURIES

ST PERPETUA, *d.* 203

THE Christian Church had been prepared to follow in the steps of its Master from the first, and persecution began with the imprisonment of St Peter. St Stephen was stoned to death, St James beheaded, St Paul hounded from city to city. But the Jewish persecution practically ceased when Jerusalem was laid waste in A.D. 70 by the Roman armies, and then it was the pagans [1] who persecuted. They did so for a number of reasons. Firstly, they regarded the Christians as sect of the Jews, whom they hated for their exclusiveness and their refusal to recognise any God but their own, or offer sacrifices to the Emperor's statue or swear by his genius (the recognised method of showing loyalty to the Empire). All this seemed like dangerous treason, and it was also bad for such trades as idol-making. Besides, to the ignorant, the Christians seemed to

[1] This word, like " heathen," is used to mean those who were not Jews or Christians.

12

be atheists, for they had no idols, and not even a temple. And, lastly, it was rumoured (falsely of course) that at the secret service they held at day-break, to which no pagan was admitted, they practised dreadful things, killing an infant and devouring it. " Haters of the human race," the pagans called them, and were ready to do them harm as soon as an opportunity offered itself.

That opportunity came in A.D. 64 when a great fire broke out in Rome, destroying the wooden buildings in the poorer part of the city, raging for a week and breaking out again, and burning nearly the whole of the palace of Augustus. A whisper ran through the city that the foul, half-insane Emperor Nero (who had already killed his wife and his mother) had started it in order to build the city again more splendidly to his own glori-fication. Another whisper ran through the city (and Nero encouraged this one) that the Chris-tians had started the fire. Tacitus, the historian, tells the dreadful story. " To get rid of the rumour, Nero put in his own place as culprits . . . the men whom the common people hated for their secret crimes and called Christians. In the first place some were seized and made to confess : then on their information a whole multitude were convicted. And they were not only put to death with insult in that they were dressed up in the skins of wild beasts to perish either by the worrying

of dogs, or on crosses, or by fire; but when day-
light failed they were burnt to serve as lights by
night. Nero had thrown open his gardens for
that spectacle and was giving a circus performance,
joining the rabble in a jockey's dress."

From the Book of the Revelation we learn that
the persecution spread farther, and from early
writings that two great Apostles sealed their faith
with their blood: St Paul was beheaded, St Peter
crucified. The great network of underground
passages found in the neighbourhood of Rome,
and called catacombs, was originally a Jewish,
then a Christian cemetery; here Christians buried
their dead, celebrated the Eucharist, and sometimes fled for safety. To this day we can see the
symbols of faith and words of hope they carved
on the tombs.

This was the first of the persecutions which
were to break out again and again during the next
three hundred years. In A.D. 107 Ignatius, Bishop
of Antioch, was condemned to be devoured by
wild beasts. In A.D. 156 Polycarp, the heroic
Bishop of Smyrna, met his death nobly, replying
to the Pro-Consul who bade him revile Christ and
burn incense to Cæsar: " Eighty and six years have
I served Him and He has done me no wrong; how
then can I blaspheme my King Who saved me?"

We have many stories of the martyrs. There
was Blandina, a slave girl, who, in the persecution

of A.D. 177, tired out all her tormentors, and would say nothing but "I am a Christian; we do nothing vile." There was Cyprian, the great teacher and writer, Bishop of Carthage, who died at the hand of the executioner with a great crowd of Christians fearlessly standing round. And there were scores of others, named and nameless.

From Carthage, too, comes the undying story of St Perpetua, told by herself and by those who saw her die.

In the year A.D. 203, when persecution broke out, she was twenty-two years old, well-born and educated, married, and with a baby son at her breast when they took her to the dark, stifling prison. She was parted from her baby at first, but she got him back for a while, "and my prison suddenly became a palace," she said. Her old father came and pleaded with her to renounce Christ. "Behold your brothers, behold your mother and your aunt; look upon your son who cannot live without you. No one of us will ever hold up his head again if anything happens to you." Perpetua stood like a rock. At the public trial she confessed openly before the judge that she was a Christian. "Then he pronounced sentence against us all and condemned us to the beasts and we joyfully went down to the prison."

The imperial prisons were kept by gaolers who were always open to bribes, and thus Christians could come and visit their friends and help and comfort them. And in the arena, between the acts, they were allowed to see and speak to their friends, and this is how we come to have so many records of what they said and did. "The day of their victory dawned, and they went forth from the prison into the amphitheatre as if to heaven, joyful, with radiant countenances." With Perpetua there was a slave girl, Felicitas, who had also just had her first baby. The two women were condemned to be tossed by a maddened cow. When Perpetua fell to the ground she drew her garments round her and tied up her dishevelled hair, for loose hair was a sign of mourning, and she was determined to die looking joyful. She took Felicitas by the hand and raised her up. They were led out of the arena. "Let not our sufferings be a stumbling-block to you," she said to her young brother who was a catechumen. Then the Christians gave each other the kiss of peace, and went back into the arena to die together. While the mob howled for their death, one of the attendants killed them with a sword.

So the splendid, awful, story goes on. The last persecution took place in the reign of the Emperor Diocletian, 284-305, and in this case the decree was issued that not only were the Christians to be put to death, but their churches were to be confiscated and their Scriptures burned. The

Roman provinces felt this persecution. Bede, the historian, tells us (though this may have happened earlier) that far away in Britain, Alban, who had sheltered a Christian priest and been converted by him, laid down his life for his Master on a flowery hill. We worship in that place, in a church called by his name, to this day.

But even this last terror did not crush out the Church. For 129 years out of 249 it had been persecuted by every means its enemies could devise, and yet the Christians grew. In the peaceful years between the periods of persecution they could teach their Faith; during the periods of persecution some were spared by the leniency of Roman governors, and in some provinces the edicts were never enforced. But, above all, every martyr was a missionary. In A.D. 197 Tertullian, one of the most famous defenders of the Faith, wrote these words, "We are a people of yesterday, and yet we have filled every place belonging to you, cities, islands, castles, towns, assemblies, your very camp, your tribes, palace, forum . . . nothing whatever is achieved by each more exquisite cruelty you invent, on the contrary it wins men for our school. We are made more as often as you mow us down. The blood of Christians is seed."

In the great battle of endurance the Church had won. In the year A.D. 313 an edict of toleration was issued, permitting Imperial subjects, including Christians, to worship as they pleased, and ordering that their confiscated churches should be restored to them. The Emperor Constantine thought he saw a fiery cross in the sky on the eve of one of his military victories, with the words HOC VINCE, " in this conquer." He dreamed that Christ bade him take the cross for a standard.

From this time forward the Emperor befriended the Church.

NOTES . . . .

THE DEFENDERS OF THE FAITH.—The martyrs proved by their joyful endurance to the end that the Faith was a better thing than life itself. It was left to those who lived on to explain to Jews and Pagans what the Faith really was. These writers are called APOLOGISTS because they wrote books which explain and justify Christianity.

When JUSTIN MARTYR wrote his *Apologies*, including a book for the Jews, the Church had few books besides the Gospels and letters from Apostles and Bishops. A little later CLEMENT of ALEXANDRIA wrote mostly for Christians. He had a broad and generous mind, and loved beauty and goodness wherever he met them, in Christian or Pagan, and he believed that the Faith ought to make people not only wise and good, but courteous and well-mannered too.

IRENÆUS wrote a book called *Against the Heresies* to condemn some wrong ideas which had crept into Christian teaching. He was probably martyred in A.D. 202.

The great African, TERTULLIAN, 160-223, who had been a lawyer, wrote a great deal, and his books are full of memorable sayings like these : " Christ our Master called Himself Truth, not Convention." " He who fears to suffer cannot be His who suffered."

ORIGEN of ALEXANDRIA (185-254) was a brilliant and daring thinker, who, among his many other books, wrote long commentaries on the Scriptures in an allegorical style. Like other brilliant people his ideas were sometimes confusing and dangerous to uneducated people, and after he died some of them were condemned by the Church.

CYPRIAN, Bishop of Carthage, and martyr in A.D. 258, wrote mostly on the government and discipline of the Church. He also wrote a book on the Lord's Prayer.

CHAPTER III
THE WAR AGAINST WORLDLINESS
Fourth Century
ST ANTHONY, A.D. 251–356

When the Church was continually faced with the possibility of loss, torture and death, every Christian knew that to follow Christ meant complete renunciation. Such people might be fanatics, but they were at least heroic and sincere. But when the persecutions ceased it became easy, and even fashionable, to profess Christianity. Great numbers of the best men and women had laid down their lives, and now the Church was flooded with new converts fresh from heathen homes and living in a heathen civilisation. The life of the cities was as bad as ever, and the result of all this was a lowering of ideals and standards and a love of ease and wealth and influential positions in the Church.

Against this attitude there arose a protest which took two forms. One set of Christians remained in the cities, under the leadership of their heroic bishops, determinedly living the Christian life in heathen surroundings ; another group fled into the Egyptian deserts, there to live a life of stern self-renunciation in the spirit in which the martyrs gave up life itself for Christ.

Even before the persecutions finally ceased, the first and perhaps the greatest of these desert-dwellers, Antony (born about A.D. 251), heard read in church the words spoken by Our Lord to the rich young ruler, and forthwith sold all his possessions and went into the wilderness. He spent thirty-five years, first in an old tomb and then in a ruined castle, in fasting, prayer, and meditation, in fighting his own evil thoughts and temptations. When the battle was won such crowds flocked to see him and ask for his healing prayers that he fled across the Nile and built a little cell by a clear spring, where he lived among the wild creatures of the desert, who became his friends. But his fame followed him; others gathered round and built their cells near, and in this way a monastery [1] grew up in that place. In these early monasteries the monks lived each according to his own rule, though there were certain hours of the day at which they all prayed, and on Saturday and Sunday they met to celebrate the Eucharist in a central church. Farther down the Nile there were other monasteries for

[1] House of Monks, a word meaning "solitaries." Women who practised this kind of life came to be called Nuns, a title of respect: their homes, nunneries. The word "convent" is used to mean either monasteries or nunneries.

men and nunneries for women of a different sort. These grew up under the guidance of the hermit Pachomius, and here men and women were graded into classes according to their spiritual development, and lived strictly according to his rule. The first monks had each cultivated his own strip of ground for food, but when they congregated in big numbers the labour had to be divided. A monk who visited the Egyptian monasteries in these times tells us : " one works on the land as a labourer, another in the garden, another in the carpenter's shop, another in the fuller's shop, another weaving the big baskets, another in the tannery, another in the shoe-maker's shop, another in the scriptorium,[1] another weaving the young reeds. And they all learn the Scriptures by heart."

The work of the monks provided them with food and clothing. They each wore a linen tunic with a rough robe over it, a small hood or cowl, a narrow cape, a woollen scarf or girdle to tie up the robe when working, and sandals. Each carried a sheepskin and a staff. If there was food left over, or profit from the sale of linen or wine or baskets which the monks made and sold, it was given to the poor peasants who lived near.

The real work of the monks was prayer and

[1] Writing-room.

self-conquest. There are strange and terrible tales of how they tried to overcome their temptations and passions. Some ate only once in five days; some rarely drank; some lived in places so small they could never stretch themselves, or on the top of tall pillars like St Simeon Stylites; some hardly ever slept. It seems to us that their methods must have often made things worse rather than better, increased temptation and weakened their resistance to it, and it is true that they often had a wrong and unchristian attitude towards their bodies, treating them as slaves and enemies, and despising marriage as something unworthy of the highest sort of Christians. But because they lived like this for a noble end, fighting against worldliness with the best weapons they knew, many of them came out of this terrible training serene and happy, able to heal and bless.

There were great teachers in the desert too; men like Macarius of Alexandria and the Abbot Isaac, who could teach their followers much about prayer and Christian living.

The fame of the monks grew and spread. Twice St Antony left the desert for the city, once to help and encourage the martyrs during a persecution, and once to help Athanasius, Bishop of Alexandria, to fight the wrong ideas which were getting mixed with the true faith. Each time men treated him with the utmost respect, and no one dared touch him. When his life was written by St Athanasius (who had visited him as a young man, and who later fled to the monasteries for safety), scores of men and women read it with joy and reverence. Nearly a hundred years later St Augustine read it and felt his heart turn to God ; nearly a thousand years later still the great scholar St Thomas Aquinas counted it among his favourite books.

Monasteries sprang up in other places—Palestine, Syria, Mesopotamia. Asia Minor, Gaul, Germany, and Ireland. From Gaul comes the story of that great soldier saint, Martin, who gave half his cloak to a beggar, and in a dream saw Christ wearing it. Martin's half-cloak became a treasure owned by kings ; the monastery he built a place of light and learning ; the book of his life, written by his disciple Sulpicius Severus, was a " best-seller " in its day.

These early monks drove two ideas deep into the mind of the Church. The first, that a Christian must be ready to renounce everything for his Master, and must maintain that readiness by discipline of body and mind. The second, that though every man will finally be judged according to his capacity and calling, the life of a monk is in itself higher than any other sort of life. The first of these ideas has never been questioned since; the second was challenged almost immediately, but it gained ground and became the general belief for the next thousand years.

NOTES   .   .   .   .

CHRISTIAN EDUCATION. — At first the only schools for advanced education open to Christians who lived in the cities were those taught by pagan philosophers; but in the last half of the second century they began to organise schools of their own. Bishops gathered their clergy and people round them and taught them, and in time these Episcopal Schools became centres of learning. PANTÆNUS was the first important teacher in the famous catechetical school at Alexandria, and other schools of this sort sprang up in the East, at Nisibis, Edessa, etc. The pupils studied theology, philosophy, literature, grammar, arithmetic, music, geometry, astronomy, and other subjects. At first Christians studied the old pagan literature, but later they grew afraid of the bad effect it might have on their minds and their lives, and in A.D. 401 the Council of Carthage forbade the clergy to use these books. The Books of the Old and New Testament were read in church, and might be studied privately on the church premises.

FAMOUS TEACHERS AND LEADERS.—Many great Christian teachers and leaders lived during the fourth and fifth centuries. EUSEBIUS of CÆSAREA, 265-340, who wrote a history of the Church; BASIL THE GREAT, 330-379, bishop and monk (who made a new Rule for monks), his brother GREGORY of NYSSA, and his friend GREGORY NAZIANZEN; CHRYSOSTOM, the great preacher and Bishop of Constantinople (347-407); JEROME, 340-420, who founded monasteries in Palestine and made a famous translation of the Bible into Latin; CYRIL, d. 444, Bishop of Alexandria, a fierce and intolerant champion of the Faith as he understood it; THEODORE of MOPSUESTIA, 350-428, who wrote commentaries on the Bible in the style of a good modern scholar; and ATHANASIUS, AMBROSE, and AUGUSTINE, about whom more is to be said.

CHAPTER IV

THE BATTLE FOR THE FAITH
Fourth Century

ST ATHANASIUS, A.D. 296-373

THE Christian Church was fighting two battles at this time. One, as we have seen, was against wickedness and worldliness; the other, equally important, was a battle for the truths of the Faith.

In the ancient world there was an idea that matter itself was evil. Those who believed this, yet wanted to become Christians, could not accept the fact that God had come to us in human flesh, so they evolved a theory that the body of Jesus which men saw and touched was not real. They also taught that Jesus Himself was not the Only Begotten Son of God, but only one of many spirits sent from Him to help and teach mankind. The Church fought these ideas from the days of St Paul and St John. This heresy [1] was called Gnosticism.

Another heresy began in the city of Alexandria, where Arius, a priest who had charge of an

---

[1] The word "heretics" is used to mean persons who accept only part of the Christian Faith.

important Church there, declared that Jesus was not really God, but something between God and man, a great demi-god, created from the beginning before time was. He said this so carefully and reverently that many Christians thought he was teaching the truth.

The old Bishop of Alexandria saw the danger at once, but he gave Arius a fair chance of stating his views, first in a private interview, then at a meeting of the city clergy, and lastly at a small council of bishops. Still Arius held to his opinions. He wrote them in verse, he made them into songs, and taught them to his followers. A great quarrel sprang up between these Arians and the rest of the Church, and spread beyond Egypt. The Emperor heard of it and wrote to Alexandria warning the Christians there not to try to settle matters too difficult for them. But the noble Spanish Bishop, Hosius, who carried the letter, saw that this affair mattered very much indeed, and when he returned he persuaded the Emperor to call a Council of Christian bishops to settle this and some other matters.

So the Council met in the city of Nicea, and for the first time in history bishops representing the whole Church gathered together, three hundred and eighteen of them, it was said. They came from Palestine and Syria, Asia Minor, Egypt, Africa, and Spain. A fair-haired Goth from the far North was there, and two priests from the Bishop of Rome, who could not come himself. There were hermits from the desert, men scarred with the tortures of the persecutions, and even some curious heathen philosophers. Arius was there, a thin dark giant of a man, white-faced and weak-eyed, with tangled hair and a rough hermit's dress. He had a wonderful voice and a fascinating way of speaking. By the side of the Bishop of Alexandria, and supporting everything he said, stood his deacon, a young man with auburn hair and a quick, brilliant way of saying things. He had been brought up by the Bishop and had been his secretary, and though still young he had already written two famous books. His name was Athanasius.

On a throne in the centre of the hall was a copy of the Gospels, and at one end of the hall a small gilt seat for the Emperor Constantine, who, in his jewelled purple robes, waited for a sign from the bishops before he sat down.

The Emperor begged for peace and charity from the start, but the arguments that followed were fierce and long, and there were a good many things to be settled. Then the Council dealt with Arius.

The Bishop of Alexandria, and those who followed him, appealed at first to the Scriptures, and to a simple creed which Eusebius of Cæsarea put forward as the one he learnt before he was baptised. But they soon saw that Arius and his followers could use the same words and mean something quite different, so they had to think of a word which expressed exactly what they meant and could not be misunderstood. What they wanted to say was that Christ was God, of the same nature, or, as they would put it, essence. At last they found a Greek word which meant just that, *homoousion*.

Now, as we saw, Christians were all taught a creed before they were baptised ; it was the same everywhere, though the wording differed a little in the different Churches. But at Nicea a testing creed was made to which every bishop had to agree, and the first part of the creed had these words in it :

I believe . . . in One Lord Jesus Christ the Son of God . . . very God from very God, begotten not made, one in essence with the Father.

Thus the Council settled the matter. Arius and his followers were banished for a time, and the book in which he had expressed his views was burned.

We have no record of what Athanasius said at the Council, but we know that from this time forward he was a famous man, admired by many, and bitterly hated by those who disagreed with him. A year after the Council he was made Bishop of Alexandria, and for a short time afterwards he visited his people and wrote books in peace ; after that his life was one long adventure and battle for the Faith. For Constantine, and the emperors who succeeded him, favoured Arius again, and bitterly persecuted Athanasius and his followers. Five times the bishop was driven into exile by the plots and false accusations of his enemies, or by hostile emperors. Once he went to Treves, once he sought the friendship and protection of the Bishop of Rome, more than once he lived as a hunted man among the monasteries of the Egyptian deserts, passed on from one place to another and closely hidden by the monks, whom he had always befriended when he was in power. From his hiding-place he sent out letters to his friends, many of whom were mourning the loss of their churches, which had been given to the Arians. Athanasius wrote, " We have the Faith, of that nothing can rob us. Every place is good where the Faith is. Wherever holy men dwell the place is holy."

Once his church was surrounded by soldiers, who interrupted the service, massacring the worshippers, and dragging out the altar and curtains to burn them in the street, and the Bishop barely escaped with his life. Once the boat in which he was escaping was chased by his enemies, who, coming alongside, enquired of the sailors where Athanasius was. "He is not far off," they replied, and the enemy sheered off and went to look for him elsewhere.

By far the worst part of Athanasius' suffering was the loss of his friends, who, one by one accepted the Arian creed, not because they really believed it, but because of the way in which they were persecuted. He was left almost alone, yet he never wavered in his faith. *Athanasius contra mundum* (Athanasius against the world), is a saying we still use to describe the hero of a lone fight.

Forty years after he had been made bishop he came back to his city for the last time, there to write and govern and name his successor and die in peace. He saw the triumph of the true Faith in the end. But his greatest triumph was achieved after his death, when the Faith for which he had fought at Nicea was embodied in a creed which has been said from that time to this day in Christian Churches throughout the whole world.

NOTES . . . .

THE COUNCILS.—The Council of Nicea was the first of a number of famous Church Councils which met to decide important matters of belief and discipline. They are spoken of as Ecumenical, or General Councils, because the whole of the

Christian Church was represented there, and are called by the names of the towns in which they met. About a century after the Council of Nicea had condemned the Arian heresy, which declared that Our Lord was not truly God, another Council (Ephesus, A.D. 431) condemned the teaching of Apollinarius and Nestorius which declared that He was not truly Man.

THE CREEDS.—Three great creeds are used in the Christian Church. The oldest and shortest is called the APOSTLES' CREED, because it expresses in a very short and simple way what the Apostles taught about God the Father, Our Lord Jesus Christ, the Holy Ghost, the Church, forgiveness, and eternal life. In many churches it is used at Baptism and in other services. The second is called the NICENE CREED, because it contains the definition of Our Lord's nature which was decided upon at Nicea, though it was put together, as we know it, at the first Council of Constantinople (381). It is longer and more detailed than the Apostles' Creed, and is used at the celebration of the Eucharist. The third is called the ATHANASIAN CREED, because, although he did not write it, it was thought to express what Athanasius believed. It was not made as a creed like the other two, but was written, we think, in the sixth century, as a hymn to be sung after the Psalms. It is only used occasionally.

CHURCH BUILDINGS AND CHURCH SERVICES.—
During these times, and for the next two or three
hundred years, church buildings became larger
and more interesting. In the East, where most
church building took place, the roofs were
crowned with domes, the pillars and walls inlaid
with wonderful mosaic pictures in gold and
colours. The rail or lattice before the altar
became a screen painted with pictures, with doors
in it through which the priest could go. The
services of the Church became more interesting
too. We know from the Service book of Bishop
Serapion, who was a friend of St Athanasius, in
what beautiful and stately language the Church
worshipped God. "We praise Thee, O unseen
Father, provider of immortality, Thou art the
fount of life, the fount of light, the fount of grace
and truth, O lover of men, O lover of the poor,
Who reconcilest Thyself to all and drawest all to
Thyself through the advent of Thy beloved Son."

One of the men who helped to bring more
beauty and order into the Church was AMBROSE,
Bishop of Milan.

CHAPTER V

THE GOVERNMENT AND DISCIPLINE
OF THE CHURCH

FOURTH AND FIFTH CENTURIES

ST AMBROSE, A.D. 340–397; ST AUGUSTINE, A.D. 354–430

AT this period in the history of the Church it is
necessary to try to understand the attitude of the
early Christians to the State.

St Paul shared with the great Roman, Cicero,
the idea that a State is a community of men who
are assembled to maintain justice; therefore, since
the purpose of civil government is good, men
ought to obey the civil authorities. " The powers
that be are ordained of God." But if the authorities do not maintain justice, and command men
to sin, then they are to be resisted. " We ought
to obey God rather than men," said the Apostles,
and the martyrs wrote that answer in blood.

Thus we find that the first leaders and teachers
of the Church, as soon as the persecutions were
over, enthusiastically supported and obeyed the
Emperor, yet dared to disobey and even rebuke
him on certain occasions. At this point they had
to face a new difficulty—not the hostility of the

Emperor, but the possibility that he would treat the Church as a sort of State department, and interfere in its belief and worship as he was accustomed to do with the pagan religions. Here the Church, especially in the West, resolutely asserted its independence. " The purple makes princes, not priests," said Ambrose, Bishop of Milan, when the Emperor, who was a Christian, was about to take his seat among the clergy in church, and His Majesty was courteously shown to another seat.

Ambrose was one of the first great leaders of the Church to take a bold stand with regard to the claims of the State. He had been brought up by Christian parents, became a lawyer, and at thirty-four years of age held the important post of consul in Milan. He was so much liked and respected that he was elected Bishop while still a consul.

The post was a difficult and dangerous one. Fierce barbarian tribes from the north, Huns, Goths, and Vandals, were moving ominously southward, and the power of the great Empire was visibly weakening. Since Constantine's death it had been divided into East and West, and even during Ambrose's life there were three Emperors on the throne of the West. He had to contend with the return of paganism, for there were those who influenced the Emperors in that direction ;

the Arian heresy, which still persisted ; and the
unjust claims of the Imperial power. When
Justina, the widow of the Emperor Valentinian,
sent soldiers in the name of her son to seize one
of the Catholic churches for the use of the Arians,[1]
Ambrose refused to give it up. " It is not the
Emperor's, it belongs to God," he replied. He
spent a whole day in one such church, surrounded
by soldiers. " We do not fight your Majesty, and
we do not fear ; we only make our prayer," was
the message he sent to the palace. The Empress
took away her soldiers.

In A.D. 390 the Emperor Theodosius had
ordered a horrible massacre to take place in the
city of Thessalonica to punish its citizens for
having murdered one of his officials. The people
were gathered into the circus as if for public
games, and then the whole defenceless crowd
killed without mercy. Not long afterwards he
proceeded in state to the church in Milan where
he usually worshipped, and was met at the door
by the great Bishop. " There is one Lord and
Emperor of this whole assembly of things," rang
out the stern voice, reminding him of One Whose
laws were more important than his own, and
in burning words forbidding him to dare to
take the Holy Sacrament with hands stained by
so much blood. Ambrose demanded that the

[1] See p. 42.

Emperor should do public penance for his crime. Theodosius refused, and for eight months avoided the Church. But when Christmas came he repented. Ambrose gave him his penance; he was to make a rule that thirty days were to elapse between the signing of a sentence of death or confiscation and its carrying out—a wise law for a hot-tempered ruler. Then Theodosius entered the church in humble penitence, dressed as an ordinary citizen of Milan, and ever afterwards was slow to revenge himself on his enemies.

Ambrose is famous not only for such actions as these, but for the books he wrote, and for some fine hymns in eight-syllabled rhymeless lines, translations of which we sing to-day. He also introduced into the church the custom of antiphonal singing, one choir answering the other across the church.

But one of the greatest things he did was to befriend a certain brilliant young teacher of Rhetoric from Thagaste in Africa, whose name was Augustine. He was the son of a pagan father and a splendid Christian mother, Monica, who was greatly troubled because he held some of the ideas of a Gnostic sect called the Manichees. Ambrose treated Augustine kindly, but did not force his teaching on him. Augustine listened to his public preaching and was impressed. At last a light broke on his mind, and in

A.D. 387 he became a Catholic Christian. He tells the whole story in his famous book of *Confessions*.

Augustine was one of the greatest and most influential thinkers and writers of the Christian Church ; his books make his readers feel as well as think. He wrote so profoundly about man's dependence on God that some later writers misunderstood him to mean that there is no free-will. This is untrue, but writers in Augustine's day were also saying exactly the opposite thing, that man is so free that he can be good without the help of God. Such was the teaching of Pelagius, a British monk, whose views Augustine fought.

Augustine's greatest book is called *The City of God*. The Empire was breaking up. In A.D. 410 Alaric the Goth had besieged and sacked the great city of Rome itself, and men were saying that it was the Christian religion which had weakened the State and called down the wrath of the gods in this terrible catastrophe. *The City of God* is an explanation and a defence of Christianity ; it describes the Church as God's city, in which dwell all His true worshippers, and against which the gates of hell shall not prevail.

Augustine was made Bishop of Hippo, in North Africa, in A.D. 395. He died there, seventy-six years old, and still faithful to this post, when the fierce Vandals were besieging the city.

NOTES   .   .   .   .

THE GOVERNMENT OF THE CHURCH.—In the New Testament, government is seen to be in the hands of the Apostles, with elders or presbyters [1] under them in charge of the local churches. A century later, we hear of Bishops [2] governing the Church, and by the end of the third century there were three clearly established orders of clergy, Bishops, Priests,[1] and Deacons. The Bishops were the rulers and teachers of the Church; they alone could consecrate new Bishops, ordain priests under them to take charge of churches and celebrate the Eucharist, and deacons to help in administrative work.

The power and authority of the Bishops varied a good deal at different times and in different places.

Each Bishop had charge of a Diocese, the centre of which was an important city. The Bishops of those cities which were very important (especially such as had been connected with an Apostle or Evangelist), came to have jurisdiction over the Bishops of lesser cities, and were called

[1] Both these words are a translation of the same Greek word PRESBUTEROS.

[2] Some Christians to-day hold that this form of government is divinely appointed, and that the line of Bishops goes right back to the Apostles themselves; this is called the theory of APOSTOLIC SUCCESSION. Others hold that it was one form of government which prevailed over others in use in the early Church, but do not think it the only right one.

Metropolitans. The Bishop of Rome had a very exalted position [1] : he had power over many provinces and was the head of the ancient capital, and the one great Church leader in the West. He was held to be the successor of St Peter, to whom the power of the keys had been given, and Roman Bishops laid more and more stress on this claim. In the East there were four of the Metropolitans, called PATRIARCHS, who were greater than the rest, those of Antioch, Alexandria, Jerusalem, and the new Imperial City, Constantinople. In A.D. 381 the Council of Constantinople gave the Bishop of that city a rank only second to that of Rome, while in A.D. 451 the Council of Chalcedon gave him the right to receive appeals from the whole Eastern Church.

Most of the Roman Bishops were wise and able men, and they both claimed and gained more power as time went on. In A.D. 445 the Emperor Valentine III declared the Roman Bishop to be the Supreme Head of the Western Church whom all his subjects must obey.

Bishops were at first elected by the clergy and laity of their own church, and elections of this kind took place during this period and later on. But as time went on their election was more and

[1] A great deal of quarrelling arose over the question whether the Bishop of Rome was the First Bishop and supreme over his own diocese—or, whether he was supreme over all the other patriarchs as well.

more often in the hands of their fellow-bishops.
The clergy were consecrated by the laying-on of
hands, anointing with oil, and prayer, thus their
ORDERS were conveyed to them, and the grace
they needed to fulfil their charge. In the fourth
century we hear of door-keepers in the church,
readers, singers, acolytes, and exorcists who drove
out evil spirits.

In these days many men entered monasteries,
and, as there were few convents for women, young
women often took vows to remain unmarried in
their homes and live a life of prayer and self-
discipline. These belonged to an Order of
VIRGINS, and wore a dark dress and a special veil.
Widows who wished to live the same kind of life
had an Order also.

CHURCH DISCIPLINE.—The Church demanded
that men should confess grave and scandalous sins
in public and do PENANCES to show their sorrow
and their willingness to amend their lives. Holy
Communion could not be received until this was
done.

Great trouble arose when consecrated bishops
and priests developed new views of the Faith,
or contradicted one another. Generally the affair
was settled by Councils. The followers of the
new views called themselves, or were called, after
their leaders, as the Arians were after Arius ; the
rest of the Church took the name CATHOLIC, which

means universal, because theirs was the original and general Christian view of things.

The first serious trouble of this kind arose over those Christians who, after Baptism, had committed grave sins or recanted the Faith, and then wished to return to the Church. Catholics took the merciful view of the case, but small parties who advocated strictness broke away from the main body of Christians, and in the fourth century a serious *schism* [1] took place under the leadership of an African Bishop named DONATUS.

[1] A break-away.

CHAPTER VI

THE SERVICE OF GOD

Fifth and Sixth Centuries

ST BENEDICT, A.D. 480–543, AND THE MONKS WHO FOLLOWED HIM

THROUGHOUT the fourth and fifth centuries the barbarian peoples had steadily gained power. The Imperial armies were hard put to it to check the raids of the fierce Vandals, the Goths, and the Huns, and from Diocletian's time small companies had been permitted to live within the Empire, whilst later, whole tribes settled within its boundaries. All this time they were being drafted into the army under their own chiefs as officers, and it was these men who finally became the masters of the Western Empire, deposing the Emperor and setting up a German, Odoacer, in his stead. The barbarians were fierce and rough, but some of them had fine qualities, and they learned from the cultured people they conquered. (Alaric, for instance, did not destroy the fine buildings of Rome when he sacked it.) Some of the barbarians had learnt the Christian faith, though many of them only knew the half-Christianity of Arius.

Theodoric, the East-Gothic King, who succeeded Odoacer in A.D. 493, though an Arian, treated the Catholics well; he was a good and wise ruler, and his chief minister, Cassiodorus (477-570) was a scholarly historian of his own and ancient times.

Though there was still a "Roman" Emperor in the East, the old power and unity of the Empire had gone, and the civilization of the West was being broken to pieces. Half-savage hordes of men swept from place to place, plundering and spoiling as they went, and it seemed to many as if the end of the world was very near.

In the year A.D. 500 an Italian of noble birth, named Benedict, made his way to a cave near one of Nero's ruined palaces at Subiaco, there to fast and pray and discipline himself like St Antony of old. Like St Antony, his fame spread, and men began to bring their sons to him to be taught. Three years later his enemies drove him from Subiaco, and, with his followers, he went to Monte Cassino, where he destroyed an old Temple dedicated to Apollo, and built his own oratory of St Martin in its place.

Here was Benedict's first monastery, and from this place there was to come an army of men who carried no swords, but whose hands were strong to push a plough, and skilful to wield a pen, and who were to become the peaceful conquerors of the barbarians and the restorers of the wasted lands of the Empire.

Benedict's monastery was unlike any other. He had come to realise that many men would gladly give themselves to the service of God as monks, leaving their property and the chance of a happy married life, but that few could undertake the terrible discipline of the old monks of the desert. So he made a Rule which any good man could keep. "We are going to establish a School for God's Service in which nothing is too hard and burdensome," he said, and he called men to his adventure thus: "To thee, whoever thou art, who renouncest thine own will to fight under the true King, thy Lord Christ, and takest into thy hands the valiant and glorious weapons of obedience, are my words addressed."

Benedict arranged that his monks should live in small families under their Abbot as their Father, whom they must always implicitly obey. They were to stay in their own monastery and not wander about as some monks did, and each monastery was to be independent, though the way of living was to be the same in all.

That way was simple and hard, but not too hard for ordinary men. The monks got up at two o'clock to pray, but they went to bed at sunset; their clothes were clean and comfortable and sensible, and made to fit; they ate all ordinary food except the flesh of four-footed animals, and for half the year they had two meals a day as other people did, though the rest of the year they had only one. For six or seven hours a day they worked in the fields or the house or the workshop, and for three they read and studied the Scriptures and the lives of the monks of the Egyptian deserts and other books. But the great work of the Benedictines was their praise and prayer in church, "the Work of God" Benedict called it, and he taught his monks to pray reverently, and to pay attention to the words they were saying. Six times in the day and once in the night they prayed together, and on Sundays they celebrated the Eucharist.

Thus Benedict and his monks lived for fifteen years, and every year he went down to the foot of the mountain where he lived, and talked to his sister Scholastica, who had organised a convent for women on very much the same lines as the monastery for men.

In A.D. 543 he died. Forty-six years later the Lombards raided Italy, and the Benedictines of Monte Cassino fled to Rome, carrying their Rule with them.

One by one, in place after place, Benedictine monasteries were built, always on the plan of a Roman country house—the buildings grouped round a courtyard, with garden and mill and

hospital and bake-house outside.   A covered walk
(the cloister) was built round the courtyard, and
was used as an open-air workroom, as well as a
place for exercise.   Each monastery had its church,
refectory (dining-room), calefactory (a room which
could be warmed), dormitory for sleeping, lavatory
for washing, store-rooms and kitchen.

The hard-working monks dug and drained the
land, felled trees and planted them, and turned
rough heaths and wild forests into golden corn-
fields and good pastures.   The people of the
place came to them for help and friendship, and
as the centuries rolled by those first simple
dwellings and peasant huts became stately abbeys
surrounded by farms and villages and towns.
The monks not only taught their neighbours the
Christian Faith, but fed them in times of famine,
for their own hard work and simple living made
them wealthy as time went on.   They opened
schools for outsiders, as well as schools for those
who were training to become monks, and they
copied and preserved the ancient writings and the
great literature of the pagans, and so helped to save
what was good from the wreck of the old world.
For some time they were the chief educators of
the people, for Justinian, the Eastern Emperor,
had closed the pagan universities in A.D. 529, and
there were few Episcopal schools in those days.
Wherever the monks went they taught men to

read and write, to build well and farm wisely, to carve and paint and gild and make things beautiful, as they themselves made their own churches beautiful to the glory of God.

The monks did not set out to be teachers or farmers or builders, but the " school for the Service of God " could not help being a " school for the Service of Man " also. Nevertheless the " work of God " was always put first, and through the day and in the early darkness the monks sang His praises in abbeys which grew more stately and beautiful, with music more pure and lovely, from books where gold and colours glowed from the parchment pages; and in so doing they showed to all those around them how real and how great was the God whom men so delighted to praise.

NOTES . . . .

THE DAY AND NIGHT PRAYERS OF THE CHURCH. —The first Christians had been brought up as Jews to pray at certain hours of the day, and when they ceased to be Jews they still kept special times for prayer. In early times they used to gather together late on Saturday night to prepare themselves for the Sunday Eucharist; afterwards these night services were held before any special holyday, and were sometimes called Vigils. By

about A.D. 300 there were morning and evening
services in the churches every day.

The monks naturally had more services than
this. By the end of the fifth century they were
accustomed to one or two during the night and
six during the day. These HOURS OF PRAYER
were called Nocturns, or Mattins (at cockcrow),
Lauds (at sunrise), Prime (before starting work),
Terce (at nine), Sext (at mid-day), None (at three
o'clock), Vespers (at sunset), and Compline (at
bedtime).

For many centuries the services of the Hours
have been said and sung (as they are still in monasteries throughout the world), and the Morning
and Evening Prayer to which the church bells
call English people to-day are only the old Hours,
a little altered and simplified, which Ambrose and
Augustine and Benedict said some fourteen
hundred years ago.

CHAPTER VII

THE MISSIONARIES TO THE WEST
Fifth, Sixth, Seventh, and Eighth Centuries

PATRICK, A.D. 389–461; COLUMBA, A.D. 521–597;
AUGUSTINE, d. 605; AIDAN, d. 651

Long before Benedict made his Rule, monasteries very like those in Egypt had sprung up in the province of Gaul, at Tours, on the Island of Lerins, and at other places. To these monasteries came travellers and pilgrims to learn the monks' way of life, to listen to the teaching of their ·founders, and to study the books which every monastery collected. The monasteries were missionary centres, and the travellers carried away the Faith with them.

In the year A.D. 412 a Briton named Patrick came to one of these, perhaps to Tours. He had been brought up a Christian, but pirates had kidnapped him as a boy and carried him away to heathen Ireland, from which, by the help of God, he had only just escaped. He was a rough, uneducated man when he came, but he stayed long enough in Gaul, partly at Lerins and partly with the great Bishop Germanus of Auxerre, to become a trained

monk and priest; and when he went back to
Britain he went as Bishop to the Irish people.
Patrick tells us in the Confession of his life how
he heard the sad call of the heathen Irish and
determined to give his life to preach Christ to
them.   They were not entirely heathen, for Bishop
Palladius had been there before him, but the fierce
Irish chiefs and their Druid priests had withstood
him, and little had been done.

Patrick's life was one long struggle and adventure among these wild people, so quick to use a
weapon and so skilled in strange magic; but he
spent thirty years there, and when he died he left
Ireland Christian, with scores of monasteries up-
holding the Faith and sending out missionaries
to many another land.

From one of those monasteries the Prince-
monk Columba sailed to the tiny island of Iona,
off the Scottish coast, there to live with his one
hundred and fifty companions in the little dome-
shaped huts that clustered round their church, in
prayer and study and book-copying and the praise
of God.   They did their own farming and fishing,
and taught the Faith to their neighbours on the
mainland.   There had been Christians in Scotland
before this, for before the end of the fourth century
a disciple of St Martin of Tours called Ninian had
built a tiny stone church in Wigtownshire and
called it after his master.   But Iona became the

great missionary centre, not only for Scotland, but also for the northern part of what is now called England.

The Faith had reached south Britain very early. There were British bishops in A.D. 314, and whilst Patrick was in Ireland his teacher, Germanus, and another Bishop had been called in to help this Church, which was puzzled by the teaching of Pelagius.[1] Hardly had these two Bishops returned to Gaul, when a great invasion of Jutes and Angles and Saxons swept over the country they had left, driving the inhabitants into Somerset and Wales and Cornwall, and across the sea to that land which came to be called after them, Brittany. South Britain became Angleland, or England, and a heathen land again.

But that great Benedictine monk, Gregory, who afterwards became Bishop of Rome (or *Pope*, as the Roman bishops came to be called), saw some fair-haired English slaves in the market-place, and was determined that they and their countrymen should receive the Faith. He said in his witty, punning way that these Angles should become Angels, that their Northumbrian land, Deira, should be saved from the wrath (de ira) to come, and that these subjects of King Aella should one day sing Alleluia. Gregory was prepared to go to England himself, but his own

[1] See p. 39.

people prevented him. Ten years later he saw his chance and took it. The Saxon king of Kent, Ethelbert, had married a Christian Frankish princess named Bertha, and to Kent Gregory sent a trusted monk called Augustine, with fifty others, to preach the Faith to the royal household. Carrying a silver cross and a wooden banner on which the Crucifixion was painted, and with his precious books (a Bible in two volumes, a Gospel book, some lives of Apostles and martyrs, and New Testament commentaries) Augustine met Ethelbert in the open air, and preached the Gospel to him. The King neither understood nor accepted the Faith, but he let the monks settle in Canterbury and make converts if they could. So they went to the little church which Bertha had built and dedicated to St Martin, and which her chaplain, Luithard, served, and from that centre they began their work. It was very slow, hard work, and it took nearly a hundred years before that part of England became Christian. But from there the Faith spread. Edwin, king of Northumbria, married Bertha's daughter Ethelburga, and she brought one of the monks, named Paulinus, to the North with her, and it was through Paulinus that Edwin and his Druid priests became Christian. Edwin was baptised on the spot where the great Minster of York now stands, and for six years Paulinus and his deacon, James, went up and down preaching and baptising.   Then the heathen King Penda swept down on Northumbria, killing the King and torturing and slaying his people. Paulinus fled south with the Queen and her children, but James, the deacon, stuck to his post.

It seemed now that all Augustine's work was destroyed and that England would become heathen again.   But a young English prince named Oswald, who had escaped from his enemies to Iona and learnt the Faith there, came back to England and bravely rallied the Northumbrians against their heathen conquerors, and won the day.   He sent to Iona for a Christian teacher, and got the monk Aidan, whose gentle humble ways made everybody love him.

Eight years later Penda rose again and killed Oswald, but he was the last of the heathen kings, and after him there was a century and a half in which England grew to be a land of great scholars and missionaries, and of saints whose names will never be forgotten.

NOTES   .   .   .   .

THE MISSIONARY MONKS OF IRELAND.—The Irish Church from the sixth to the eighth century was famous for its missionary monks and the schools from which they came, *Armagh* and *Aran*, *Clonard* and *Benchor*, *Clonfert* and *Lismore*.   The

Irish were especially good at music and mathematics, they loved Greek, and they copied books in a beautiful round hand and decorated them with marvellous intricate patterns. These men went out as missionaries to Gaul and Germany, England, Norway and Iceland, taking with them their special customs, their severe way of living, their own method of dating Easter, and their manner of shaving the whole of the front part of their heads. The names of some of the greatest Irish Christians were BENIGNUS, the disciple of Patrick, and BRIDGET his friend, and FINIAN and CIARAN, COMGALL and BRENDAN, MOLUA and MOCHUDA. There was COLUMBANUS, too, and his friend GALL, who preached in Gaul and Burgundy and Italy, and founded monasteries which became famous for their learning.

THE GREAT ENGLISH SCHOOLS.—Before the Saxons came there had been famous schools in Britain, too, especially in the West, and later, when the Saxons were converted, schools sprang up in other parts of the country. There was *Lindisfarne*, which Aidan founded, where the famous monk CUTHBERT lived, and where CEDD and CHAD were trained; *Whitby* and *York* and *Ripon*; *Canterbury* and *Malmesbury* and *Sherborne*, *Evesham* and *Pershore*; *Exeter*; *Wearmouth* and *Jarrow*, and others. The last two were founded by BENEDICT BISCOP, who brought over French masons to build in stone, and put French coloured glass in the windows. He gave them pictures too, and a wonderful library of books which he spent his life collecting; and he got JOHN, the Arch-Chanter of St Peter's at Rome, to come over and teach the monks music. It was at Jarrow that BEDE, greatest of English scholars, spent the whole of his life as monk and priest, teacher and author and translator, giving us, among the one hundred and fifty books he wrote, his famous Church History.

At Whitby the ABBESS HILD ruled a double monastery of men and women, as EADBURGA did at Wimborne, and ETHELDREDA at Ely. At Whitby CÆDMON wrote the first English poetry, and here in A.D. 664 was held the Synod, when England, largely influenced by WILFRID of Ripon, decided to follow the Roman customs instead of the Irish, and thus linked her life with the life of the great Church of the West.

To Canterbury in A.D. 668 came THEODORE OF TARSUS, a Greek monk, to be its Archbishop and to make all England one, divided into Bishoprics. He brought interesting books with him, by Homer and Josephus and St Chrysostom.

And at Exeter was trained the monk BONIFACE, who went out to preach to the heathen in Friesland (Holland), and became the great missionary Bishop of Germany. Boniface came from a

Benedictine monastery, he made all the monasteries of Germany Benedictine, and he called out some of the best men and women in England to help him in his work. So BURCHARD and LULLUS and WINIBALD and WILLIBALD went out, and among the women CHUNIHILT and BERATHGILT, THEKLA and WALBURGA and LIOBA, to establish convents to teach the German women, and to copy out the books which Boniface was always wanting. Lioba was his special friend; she had written to him ever since she was a girl, and kept in touch with him all his life till he died a martyr's death at the hands of the savage Frisian people. She was buried side by side with him in the great church at Fulda, twenty-four years later. But she lived long enough to give friendship and counsel to another great man who was trying to establish the Faith in Europe—the Emperor CHARLEMAGNE.

CHAPTER VIII
A CHRISTIAN EMPIRE IN EUROPE
Ninth and Tenth Centuries
CHARLEMAGNE, A.D. 742–814; ALCUIN, d. 804

WE saw that when the barbarian tribes began to invade the Empire they often learned the Faith through those they conquered; the old civilisation might perish, but the Church went on. But in the seventh century a new and terrible danger appeared; the followers of the Prophet Mohammed swept across the world converting men to their faith or putting them to death. Syria, Arabia, Egypt, North Africa and Spain became part of their vast Empire, and in A.D. 732 they had crossed into Gaul. At Tours that year there was fought one of the most important battles in all history, when Charles the Hammer, Prime Minister to the Frankish Christian King, beat his foes and rolled back the tide of invasion that threatened Europe. His son, Pippin, got himself proclaimed King, being the first ruler to appeal to the Pope to sanction his kingship, and was anointed with holy oil by Boniface, Bishop of Germany.

When Pippin's son, Charlemagne, came to the

throne, he ruled over the countries that are now France, Belgium, the Netherlands, and Western Germany; and during his reign he extended his kingdom over the Saxons in Germany and the Lombards in Italy, the North of Spain, and some of the Slav peoples in the East.

The Eastern Empire was at this time in the hands of a woman whom the Pope would not acknowledge as ruler, and on Christmas Day in the year A.D. 800, when Charlemagne had come to Italy to help him settle a dispute, Leo held a great service of Thanksgiving in the Church of St Peter, during which he set a crown on the Frankish King's head, and proclaimed him Emperor of the Romans. Thus arose what came to be called the Holy Roman Empire.

History and legend tell us great tales of the heroic King, and of his Western Empire. But Charlemagne was not only a great soldier and ruler; he was, above all else, a Catholic Christian, and wherever he conquered, he demanded that his foes should not only accept his rule, but the Christian faith as well. Whole tribes were quite accustomed to following their leaders in matters of religion in this way in those times, but naturally a religion accepted like this did not mean much to those who took it over. They took it for what they could get out of it, and there is a story of a conquered chief in Charlemagne's reign who got himself baptised twenty times in order to collect a number of those nice white robes which the Church provided for its converts !

But Charlemagne was not content for his people to be merely baptised : he was determined that they should be properly taught too. He found things in a bad way ; in the continual wars and raids many of the best monasteries had been destroyed or had lost their books and teachers, and ignorant and unchristian men had been appointed bishops. King Pippin and Chrodegang, Bishop of Metz, had done something to make things better, but an immense task lay before Charlemagne. He began by getting the best scholars he could find to help him—Paulinus of Cæsarea, and Warnefrid, secretary to the Lombard kings, who had written a history of his own people. Warnefrid hated Charlemagne at first, and stirred up rebellions against him, but the Emperor saved him from the punishment due to traitors : " We shall not easily find another hand that can write history," he said. So Warnefrid came to the Court and taught Greek to Charlemagne's daughter, and helped to establish schools, and finally became a Benedictine monk. In A.D. 781 the Emperor found Alcuin, an English monk from the York school, journeying to Rome, and persuaded him to be his chief religious minister, to teach himself and his family and to train teachers for work in the Empire.

One of Charlemagne's greatest battles can be called the Battle for the Books. In those dark and troubled times, when so many books had been destroyed and so many good scholars killed or driven into exile, it was difficult to find any copy of the Scriptures or the Service books of the Church which had not been defaced or copied by half-educated men who had made mistakes on every page. Those who read them could hardly understand them, and those who listened only heard a jumble of meaningless words. The fine music which had been made at Rome for the services had been corrupted too. So Alcuin's first task was to make correct copies of the Scriptures and the Service books, and when these were made they were passed on to educated monks who made more copies. It took over seven years to correct the Bible, and Alcuin made it his coronation present to Charlemagne in A.D. 800.

Alcuin and the Emperor took immense pains to get the books written properly, and the monks of those times developed a beautiful, little, neat round book-writing which everyone could read. In the meantime Charlemagne got two chanters from Rome to teach the music correctly, and established music-schools at Metz and Soissons, to which all choir-masters had to send up their books for correction. The Franks found the music difficult: even in the next century a writer tells how they rolled their heads about and opened their mouths wide and made noises "like carts on a high road"! But they mastered the music in the end.

Besides correcting books Alcuin taught the Palace School — Charlemagne, his sons and daughters, his counsellors Adalhard and Angilbert, Eginhard (who afterwards wrote Charlemagne's life), and the sons of nobles and freemen whom Charlemagne collected round him for this purpose. He also revived or founded schools all over the Empire in connection with the great monasteries, such as Corbey and Orleans, St Gall and Fulda, and St Omer. Each monastery had a "little school" where any Christian could learn the Faith and prayers and music of the Christian Church, the Psalms, the way to find Easter, and some Latin grammar; it also had a "greater school" divided into two, one for monks and one for outsiders, where more difficult subjects, such as astronomy and arithmetic and music and literature, were taught. These schools collected books, and were proud of owning a Homer or a Virgil, besides the Scriptures and the writings of the Fathers of the Christian Church. Charlemagne had two scholars, Smaragdus and Theodulf of Orleans, who wrote Latin grammars for the schools. Theodulf wrote the hymn we sing on Palm Sunday, "*All glory, laud, and honour*," and he was one of the men the Emperor appointed to

c*

travel up and down the Empire hearing complaints and righting wrongs.

In the meantime Charlemagne himself was busy issuing his little laws, or "capitularies," ordering the clergy to gather the children round them and teach them; telling peasants to learn the Church music by singing it as they drove their cattle to and fro; getting more and better work out of lazy bishops, and even beginning to make a grammar of the Old German language which both he and the English then spoke. He would not let his beloved Alcuin go back to England for good, though Alcuin would have loved to end his days at York; but he let him retire to the monastery of Tours in A.D. 796, where he lived peacefully for eight years longer among the busy book-copying monks.

Ten years later the great Emperor died too. For a while the schools went on with their splendid work; then the wars between Charlemagne's sons, the feuds between the great nobles whom he had created to defend the Empire, and the coming of the Huns and the Northmen, brought ruin and desolation again.

But the Battle of the Books had won something that was never quite lost afterwards, and the muddle and ignorance which faced Charlemagne when he came to the throne was never so bad again.

NOTES . . . .

KING ALFRED OF WESSEX.—In the later days of Charlemagne and afterwards, the terrible Northmen swept down on England, plundering, burning, destroying and slaying, and wiping out almost every one of the famous monasteries and schools which had been the glory of the land. Burned homes and wasted harvests, the best Christian folk killed or scattered, and a beaten and almost weaponless people were King Alfred's heritage. No Christian ruler ever put up a better fight against such desperate odds. All English history books tell how he beat the Danes and forced them back beyond Watling Street, how he created one national law out of the varying folk-customs, and saw justice done to the poor. He encouraged noblemen and freemen to get learning for their sons, and learned enough Latin himself to translate books for his people, creating the first Anglo-Saxon literature and history, and adding to his translations his own thoughts and any new knowledge that came to him. In the struggle for Christian life and learning in England there were only six Englishmen to help him—PLEGMUND the Hermit, WEREFRITH, Bishop of Worcester, two Mercian priests, DENEWULF of Wessex, and ASSER, a monk of St David's monastery, who gave him six months' service every year. Besides these

there came to him two Frankish monks, GRIM-
BALD of St Omer, who set up a little school near
Oxford, and JOHN of Corbey, who brought a few
French monks over and settled at Athelney.   It
was these few men who, under the King, built
up again the Christian Faith and the Christian
character in England.   Asser has written for us
the aim of the King's noble life, " to leave the
men that came after him a remembrance of good
works," and the story of how he promised the
half of his days and nights to the service of God
in prayer and praise.   For all his busy days, the
King went regularly to his Mass [1] and sang and
said the Day Hours of the church, and often broke
his night's rest to go off quietly into a church to
pray.   He was a fine ruler, a soldier and a scholar ;
but above and behind all that, he was one of the
best Christians of his own and of all time.

Some of Alfred's work was carried on by
DUNSTAN (*d.* 988), Abbot of Glastonbury, Archbishop of Canterbury, artist-craftsman and counsellor of kings, who revived and reformed monastic
life in England.

---

[1] One of the names given to the Eucharist.

CHAPTER IX

THE CHURCH IN THE BYZANTINE EMPIRE

NINTH TO ELEVENTH CENTURIES

CYRILL, d. 869; METHODIUS, d. 885

WHILE the power of the Popes grew, and Frankish kings reigned in the Western Empire, the real successors of the old Romans continued to rule the East from Constantinople. Justinian I (527-565) had reconquered much lost territory, including Italy itself, poured great wealth into his capital, built the glorious Church of the Holy Wisdom (St Sophia) in the Eastern manner, and made a famous Code from the old Roman laws, which is still the basis of the laws of most civilised peoples to-day. After his reign the Lombards, the Avars, the Bulgars, the Persians, and the Saracens threatened the ruin of the Empire again, and Constantinople was twice besieged by the Mohammedans, but not taken.

In 867 a strong Emperor, Basil the Macedonian, came to the throne and began to reconquer his foes. The Eastern Empire, which is often called the *Greek or Byzantine Empire*, had by this time become really Greek in thought and language, and its people grew steadily more hostile to the Westerns (Latins) and to the claims of the Popes. Fierce quarrelling arose over the use of statues in the churches, and the addition of three words to the Nicene Creed,[1] and came to a head when Bishop Ignatius was deposed for courageously condemning the sins of an Eastern Emperor, and Photius was put in his place. Both Bishops appealed to the Pope, who decided in favour of Ignatius, and condemned Photius. Photius was very angry, and wrote a letter to the Eastern Bishops accusing the Western Church of heresy, and this was the beginning of a bitter quarrel which finally divided the Church into East and West.

In the meantime the peoples who conquered or were conquered by the Empire were coming into touch with the Christian faith. They often heard it first from ignorant men (for the Church had never had enough good teachers), and they often saw Christian rulers in Church and State living bad lives; but they also saw something of its goodness and beauty in the lives of those who were Christians in more than name. Again and again tribal princes would send to Pope or Emperor for someone to teach them the Christian faith.

[1] See p. 72.

In these days great difficulties were beginning to arise over the problem of languages. The West still used Latin officially, and in the Church services, though prayers and creeds and Scriptures were being translated for private use. England, Gaul, Germany, and Scandinavia spoke Teutonic languages and could understand one another, though the Celtic spoken by the Welsh and Irish and Scots had to be translated to them. The Eastern Empire talked Greek, but those lands north of Greece and west of Germany, including the vast country of Russia, could understand nothing but Slavonic.

It was from these regions in 858 that the Prince of the Avars sent to Constantinople begging for Christian teachers. The Emperor sent them two brother monks—Cyrill, a priest, who had been educated by Photius and had once been the palace librarian, and Methodius, who had been an artist and a soldier and had once governed the Græco-Slavonic province of Pannonia.

After working for a little while among the Avars, the two brothers went down into the Crimea and began the great task of translating the Scriptures into the Slavonic tongue, and they had to invent an alphabet before they could do it. Four years later another appeal for Christian teachers came from the Slav peoples, and again the brothers set out together.

On his way Methodius was called to the court
of Bulgaria to paint a hunting picture for the
Prince. " Let it be a good picture, large and
terrible," he said. Methodius promised to paint
it if he could be left entirely alone to do it. But
when it was finished, and the Prince entered his
palace hall, he saw, not a hunting scene, but a
great Doom-picture, Christ on His throne judging
good and evil men on the Last Day. " What
does it mean ? " asked the Prince, and Methodius
told him. Walking up to the picture the Prince
bowed his head before it, and then said to the
artist, " Take me and teach me, that I too may
pass to the beautiful side of the picture."

Cyrill and Methodius stayed and preached the
Faith to the Bulgars, and then went north into
Moravia. Here the jealousy of the neighbouring
German princes, who belonged to the Western
Empire, hindered their work, and the princes
complained of them to the Pope because they said
Mass in Slavonic instead of Latin. The Pope
called the brothers to him and questioned them
about their work, but he found only two good
Christians and fine missionaries, and he gave them
leave to go back with full permission to go on
with what they were doing.

Here at Rome Cyrill died, but Methodius went
back and became Bishop of Pannonia, and later
of Moravia. The jealous German priests and

princes would not let him alone, but the real goodness and sincerity of Methodius won every time. He was driven into banishment, but recalled by the Pope; called up to Rome as a heretic, but acquitted, and sent to Constantinople accused of treason, only to come back loaded with gifts and honour. At the end of his life his enemies turned the Prince of Pannonia against him, but they could not stop his work. The Faith spread among the Slav peoples from Dalmatia to the borders of Poland, and through Methodius' teaching the Duke of Bohemia became a Christian.

In 988, one hundred and three years after the death of Methodius, King Vladimir of Russia, thrilled by the glory and beauty of the worship in the Church of St Sophia, accepted the Christian faith, and for the teaching of the great people over whom he ruled there was brought to him the Scriptures which had been translated by the faithful and heroic brothers, Cyrill and Methodius.

NOTES   .   .   .   .

THE EASTERN ORTHODOX CHURCH.—The quarrels between Greeks and Latins grew worse as time went on. In 1053 the Pope excommunicated the Bishop of Constantinople, and he, together with the other Eastern bishops, declared that the Western Church was heretical, and the Eastern the only true ORTHODOX [1] Church, since when it has been called by that name. The East had protested, quite rightly, that the West had no right to make an addition [2] to the Nicene Creed without consulting them, and (though they afterwards admitted that they did not disagree with the West about what these words meant) they have ever since refused to say them. They objected also to many Church customs which had grown up in the West, among them the law that all clergy must remain unmarried. But what really lay at the back of all the quarrels was national feeling and political jealousy, and the fact that the Greeks both thought and spoke in a different language from the Latins.

In parts of Turkey and Austria, in Asia Minor and Palestine and Syria, in Egypt and Greece and Russia, the Orthodox Churches, governed by the four great Patriarchs, and the Bishops under them, proclaimed the Christian faith. Their priests were allowed to do some of the things which only a bishop might do in the West, and lay-people had more share in Church government. Each country celebrated the Eucharist in its own language, though they all used an old form of the service which had been written down by St Basil

[1] Of-the-right-opinion.

[2] The word FILIOQUE (and the Son) after " proceeding from the Father," was added at a Spanish Council in 780, in honour of Our Lord and to combat Arian ideas.

or St Chrysostom, and they all used ordinary bread, not the unleavened bread which was used in the West. Their monks followed the Rule of St Basil, not St Benedict, and their clergy followed the old custom which allowed all but bishops to marry. Their churches were built (as they still are) in the Eastern style, which has already been described.

But excepting these, and some smaller differences, the Orthodox Churches were very like the Catholic Churches [1] in the West, accepting the great creeds and the doctrines approved by the first seven general Councils, keeping the same great feasts and fasts, and having the same orders of clergy. Though the first sad break in the unity of the Church had been made, East and West were still alike enough in their ways to understand each other's faith and worship.

BYZANTINE PAINTING.—For over a hundred years (722-842) there was a great quarrel over the use of statues or images in churches, and fierce rioting and image-breaking took place. The Easterns, for the most part, felt that images were dangerous because the new barbarian converts might think they were idols and worship them. At last it was generally agreed that images might

[1] Though they took the name " Orthodox," it is better to think of the two Churches as Eastern Catholics and Western Catholics.

be used and honoured, but must not be worshipped.
The Eastern Church, however, to this day uses
no images in church except the crucifix, but
makes great use of holy pictures and mosaics
and ikons.

From very early days the Church had taught
by means of symbols and pictures. The Byzan-
tines developed the art of painting, and made very
strict rules about what should be painted, and
exactly how it should be done. (Methodius knew
how to paint his Doom-picture from memory.)
In the wealthy days of the Empire Scriptures were
often written in gold on purple-stained vellum,
and pictures painted in them, done in thick, bright
paints on squares of burnished gold-leaf. Some
of the paintings and mosaics in the Eastern
churches have a wonderful dignity and grandeur
about them, a sense of mystery and awe ; we feel
what the artist is trying to say to us, even when the
faces are ugly and the figures stiff and wrongly
drawn. In time Byzantine painting grew poor
and mechanical, but not before it had inspired the
great painters of the West to use their art in the
service of the Church.

CHAPTER X
TEMPORAL AND SPIRITUAL POWER
TWELFTH CENTURY
ST BERNARD OF CLAIRVAUX, 1091–1153

THE two centuries which followed the death of Charlemagne were dark and terrible. The Western Empire broke up, and was ruled by a French King and an Emperor of Germany and Italy (who called himself Charlemagne's successor), but it was mostly in the hands of the dukes who had been created to defend it. Each of these dukes was independent, and spent his life making war on his neighbours. Their great stone castles were surrounded by lands worked by serfs, who were little better off than slaves; and each duke had vassals and subvassals under him, who held smaller castles and lands in his domain, and paid for them by military and other services. When no wars were in progress these men held mock wars or tournaments, in which many brave men were killed. The records of the times are full of horrible tales of slaughter and torture, and there was only one voice which protested against it all —the voice of the Christian Church.

In Southern France Church Councils tried to limit and control the fights between the dukes and their vassals by a law called the TRUCE OF GOD, which commanded men to cease fighting in Lent and on four days of the week, not to attack monasteries, clerics, pilgrims or women, and to leave the poor serfs and their work in peace. If anyone broke the Truce, priests were forbidden to bring him the sacraments, and Christians to visit him when he was ill. The Truce must have been broken very often, but the ideals which lay behind it gradually soaked into men's consciences. When we use the word " knight " to-day, we think of chivalry and courtesy and purity, as well as courage ; but we often forget that these ideals were inspired in the old fighters of the West by the Christian Church.

To one of those knights whom the Church had begun to teach nobler and gentler ways—the yellow-haired Tesselin of Burgundy—a son was born in 1091, and named Bernard. The little boy grew up among his warrior brothers, rather delicate, and very clever. As a child he must have heard stories of the First Crusade, when Christian soldiers went out to protect pilgrims to the Holy Sepulchre, and rescue the Holy Land from the Turks ; and he may have gone with his father to see the body of the Duke of Burgundy, which had been brought back from Palestine to

rest in the monastery of Citeaux not far away.
Two kinds of life called to Bernard—the life of a
warrior-knight like his father and brothers, and
the life of a monk. He chose the life of a monk.
But he did not go to the monastery alone; in his
glowing enthusiasm he collected others round
him, and in 1113 he rode to the door of the monks
of Citeaux with thirty companions.

These monks lived very strictly. Their monastery had been founded by men who had left
the rich Abbey of Cluny because they felt the life
there had become too easy. Their abbot was an
Englishman, Stephen Harding. Two years after
Bernard and his friends had entered Citeaux it
had become too small for the community, and he
was one of those chosen to go out and found a
new monastery.

He built his first rough shelters in a deep-wooded
valley called Clairvaux, with a stream running
through it, and later he became abbot there. Like
Antony and Benedict and many another monk,
Bernard fought his first battle with himself, and
learned the secret of power in the great ways of
prayer. Like them, his fame spread abroad; men
talked of his wonderful sermons and writings and
the miracles he performed; and it was not long
before abbots and bishops and even kings and
popes called him from Clairvaux to help them.

In 1129 he sat at the Council of Troyes and

encouraged and helped the Knights Templars, a band of soldiers who lived under a religious rule and were pledged to defend pilgrims to the Holy Land. From 1130 onwards he was at other Councils, too, and travelling all over France and Italy in the service of the Church, defending the cause of the true Pope against a rival who had set himself up, and persuading Henry I of England and the Emperor Lothair of Germany to his way of thinking.

Back at Clairvaux the famous, the wise, and the good came to visit him, and from there he wrote letters to some of the most important people in Christendom—the Pope, the Queen of Jerusalem, bishops in France and England, besides many another less-known friend. Many of these are great letters, full of wisdom, and always fearless. Bernard was not afraid to tell the Pope that he was interfering too much and ought to let the local bishops manage things, or to condemn his luxurious clothes and the corruption at his court. He dared to make peace between men savage enough to burn their enemies alive, and he blazed up in anger against those Christians who had begun to persecute and ill-treat the Jews. In 1146, at the command of the Pope, he called men, in burning words, to the Second Crusade, and they went out in thousands. Two years after he was travelling about France again, persuading people to turn away from the false teaching of men who, it seemed to him, were trying to destroy the Catholic faith. Not many years before this he had put to silence the great scholar, Abelard,[1] and men listened to his words with reverence and awe.

The Second Crusade failed terribly, and for a while his countrymen blamed Bernard for his preaching of it. One by one his friends died, and at last, among the sorrowing monks of Clairvaux, the great Abbot passed away, saying, " Thy will be done." A knight's son and a simple monk, he had become the counsellor of the world's rulers, and more than once the real leader of Europe, not because of birth or position or any man's favour, but because his strong, incorruptible Christian life had made him the greatest man of his time.

NOTES

CHURCH ARCHITECTURE IN THE WEST.—By this time many of the Western churches were being built in the shape of a cross, with a low tower where the arms met. Inside, the massive pillars supported round arches, sometimes richly carved, and ribs of stone sprang from the walls to support the roof. The savage Northmen who invaded

[1] See p. 98.

Gaul settled there and became Christians, and when William the Norman (Northman) conquered England, his followers built these " Norman " churches in England.

THE POPES AND THE RULERS OF EUROPE.—After the Pope had crowned Charlemagne and his German successors in the West, serious quarrels arose over the rights of Church and State. One of the worst was about investitures. Bishops and abbots, often very rich through the gifts of Christian people, held their land as vassals of kings and dukes as other men did, and a bad custom had arisen by which the over-lord not only invested his vassal with the right to the land, but also chose him, and gave him the symbols of his spiritual authority, the ring and crozier. All sorts of men were thus made bishops at the will of the rough Frankish chiefs, and money changed hands in such a way that bishoprics and abbacies were really bought and sold. Even the election of the popes at one time fell into the hands of Italian political parties, and at another into the power of the German Emperor.

In 1059, however, Pope Nicholas put an end to this by decreeing that in future the Pope must only be elected by the chief Roman clergy (who came to be called *Cardinals*) ; [1] and in 1122 the

[1] Cardinals do not now have to live in Rome, though they are still the Vicars of Roman churches.

problem of investiture in Germany was settled, the Church giving the Bishop his spiritual authority, his over-lord granting him the right to his possessions.

Further troubles arose over the money which the Pope demanded from all countries to support the great Church organisation of which he was head. We saw that when the Roman Empire began to break up the Church remained the one steady united body of people in a turbulent world, and in consequence it gradually took over many of the duties of the old government. The Church saw to it that men kept their contracts, that the wills of the dead were carried out, that marriages and burials were properly undertaken, and that some protection and help were given to widows and orphans and to the poor. For a long time Churchmen were the only educated people, the only teachers. The Papal court (*curia*) was the final court of appeal for all Christians. It was supported by revenues from the Pope's lands, and also from the tithes or taxes paid by Christians in all countries, and these tithes were often felt to be burdensome by the people and their rulers, especially as they saw bishops and abbots and the Pope's special officials (*legates*) growing rich and powerful at their expense. The rulers of Europe objected also to the way in which the Church was beginning to use its power. This power was shown especially in acts of *excommunica-tion*, by which guilty persons were forbidden to receive the sacraments, and were shut off from the help and society of their fellow-Christians. Sometimes whole districts or countries were put under an interdict,[1] which meant that a great number of the privileges of the Church were denied to everyone for a time. Whilst everybody agreed that the Church had a perfect right to punish those who broke its laws, we must remember that everyone in Europe belonged to the Church, and that if a ruler was excommunicated this meant that his subjects could not associate with him, and therefore need not obey him! This gave the Pope the power to interfere with and override the rule of any prince. It was GREGORY VII who first definitely asserted that the rule of the Pope was supreme in this sense, and from his time onwards the popes became like political rulers involved in wars and intrigues with the other rulers of Europe. Thus Church and State each struggled to get all the power for itself. In England, men like ANSELM (1033-1109) and BECKET (1118-1170) fought for the independ-ence of the Church, but in many places people were so shocked at the sight of rich, greedy bishops and worldly and wicked churchmen, that

[1] There was an Interdict in the reign of King John of England.

they were almost ready to turn away from the Church itself.   In these days was born a man who was to lead many men and women back to the old, high, noble ways of Christianity.   His name was FRANCIS OF ASSISI.

CHAPTER XI

THE FRIARS

THIRTEENTH CENTURY

FRANCIS OF ASSISI, 1182-1226

FRANCIS was the son of a rich merchant of Assisi, an Italian town, a brave, gay, generous lad, who loved a good feast and fine clothes and a rousing song. He looked forward to a life of knightly glory, and he was on his way to join the Papal army which was trying to keep the Germans out of Sicily, when a strange dream and an inner voice of warning changed his whole life. He went back to Assisi quieter and more thoughtful; he would often go away into lonely places to pray, and he began to notice and be sorry for the wretched beggars who thronged the city streets. Once, during a pilgrimage to Rome, he changed clothes with a beggar and stood all day asking for alms, to see what it felt like to be really poor. From that time onwards he felt he really understood the poor, and back at Assisi he grew even more generous and sympathetic. He knew what hurt these men and women more than their poverty and wretchedness—the fact that people despised and shrank from them. This thought flashed vividly across his mind one day when he was going to throw some money to a leper, and he put it gently into his hand instead, kissed the hand courteously, and then flung his arms round the man in sympathy and love. After that he made a point of visiting and helping the lepers at their settlement not far from the town.

One day when Francis was praying in the tumble-down Church of St Damian, a voice seemed to speak to him from the great crucifix there: "Francis, go and repair my Church, which, as thou seest, is wholly a ruin." "Gladly, Lord, I will repair it," he answered. He began by giving money to the priest who served the church, but his father violently protested against this, and all that his son was now doing. Francis had heard the call of Christ, and there was nothing for him to do but make a clean break with his old life. In the presence of the friendly Bishop Guido of Assisi he gave back all the money he had taken for the church, and even the very clothes he wore. From that day he went moneyless and fatherless, dressed in an old peasant's garments on which he had marked a cross, finding and begging stones with which to rebuild the ruined Church of St Damian, whose priest shared his own simple food and shelter with him.

He repaired three other churches, and lastly the

little Church of St Mary of the Angels, in a wood not far from the city. It was in this church, which he loved best of all, that he heard the Gospel read which tells of Our Lord's commands to His Apostles : " Go forth, preach . . . possess not gold or silver . . . when you come into a house salute it, saying, Peace . . . when they deliver you up take no thought how or what to speak." On these words Francis founded his Order of Friars, a band of men who were to go about moneyless and weaponless, preaching the peace of God, and listening to His voice to tell them what they should say. They dressed in the rough, undyed stuff that peasants wore, with a rope girdle and sandals.

Francis' comrades in his great adventure were the sons of rich merchants such as Bernard of Quintavalle, farmers' sons like Giles, scholars like Peter Cathani, priests like Sylvester, a poet named Pacifico, Morico, who had served the lepers, and Leo, who could write. They lived at first in rough shelters in the wood near St Mary of the Angels, and spent their time in prayer and preaching and the care of lepers. They did work in the fields, or in the citizens' houses, to earn their bread, or begged it when no work was to be had. They went about joyfully singing to the people of the praise of God as well as preaching.

Their way of living at first startled those who

could only think of monks as grave-faced men shut up in monasteries ; but fortunately, the Pope and other far-seeing men of the time guessed of the good which such a band of men might do, and the Order was sanctioned at Rome. They were called the Friars Minor, or Little Brothers, because they would accept no high positions in the Church, but lived in great simplicity and friendliness among themselves and with the common people. Their goodness and sincerity made people listen to them and like them, and they were trusted by all because they wanted neither money nor honours.

The Franciscans went out as missionaries to Germany and Hungary and France and Spain and Syria and England, where the first house they lived in (at Canterbury) may be seen to-day. Francis went to the Holy Land, and there he went across into the lines of the enemy and preached the Gospel to the Sultan himself, who did him no harm, but sent him back in peace and safety.

In Italy the first Franciscan nunnery was established with the gentle Lady Clare as its Abbess ; and among those men and women whose families and responsibilities prevented them from joining the Franciscans, there arose a Third Order which included all who wished to live in the spirit of it as nearly as they could. One of the first of these

4

was the Lady Giacoma, the wife of a noble of old and famous family, a brave, strong-minded, generous friend of the Friars, whom Francis laughingly called *Brother* Giacoma.

Thus the Franciscans influenced the world, and it was thus that Francis most truly obeyed the command, " Rebuild my Church." Those who collected the stories of his life tell us how he loved all created things, and of how shy, wild creatures would come to him without fear, so that he could tame the savage wolf of Gubbio as well as savage mountain thieves. They speak of his thoughtfulness and courtesy in helping people ; of his joyfulness, especially when he made the " Song of the Sun," which is a praise of everything God had made ; of the great prayer and vision which left him marked with the wounds of Christ; and lastly, of his death at sunset in the early days of October as he lay at St Mary of the Angels, with a flock of larks singing marvellously outside.

There were sad troubles in the Order afterwards, some of which began in Francis' lifetime, a relaxation of the Rule, and the loss of his ideal of poverty. But the memory of him, and the story of his life, has led thousands to a truer following of his Master and Lord.

NOTES . . . .

HERESY AND THE DOMINICANS.—Before Francis'
time there had been others who, shocked at the
evil lives of many of the Church leaders, had tried
to set the world right by living a life of poverty
and prayer and good deeds. Among these the
most famous was Peter Waldo of Lyons, who,
like St Francis, gave away all his money and
lived on alms, preaching to the poor and helping
them. Both the Waldensians and the Albigensians [1]
preached against the evil customs and corrupt
clergy of their times, but they also condemned or
refused to obey the Church authorities, believing
that they had no right to the power they claimed.
The Albigenses also preached some doctrines
which were really contrary to the Christian faith.

The story of the persecution of these men and
women is very sad and terrible. We ought to
realise that the Catholics of these times thought
of those who denied the Catholic faith and despised its leaders, as criminals—men who were
fighting against God and the civilisation which
the Church had done so much to build up since
the fall of the Roman Empire. But this does not
excuse the terrible cruelty of the persecution which
took place when, in 1208, the Pope sent an army
into Southern France to suppress the heretics by

[1] So called because they lived near the city of Albi in France.

killing them wholesale and ruining their country.
Heretics had been punished by death before,
though, from the beginning, there had been some
Catholics who had protested against these methods
as unchristian and wrong ; St Martin of Tours
was one of them.

So also in these days there was a protest, this
time from a Spanish scholar named DOMINIC
(1170-1222). Dominic founded an Order of Friars
Preachers, poor and free like the Franciscans, who
went about peacefully persuading people of the
truths of the Faith. One of his famous followers
was BLESSED JORDAN OF SAXONY. Unlike the
Franciscans, the Dominicans had to be trained
scholars, quick to understand the difficulties in
men's minds, and able to explain matters simply
and clearly. They wore a white under-robe and
a black cloak. Dominic is said to have helped
people to say their prayers by counting a string
of beads, which is called a Rosary : for each bead
there was a special thought and prayer, and the
touch of the beads was meant to remind those who
prayed of what they were doing. The Rosary
has been used as a way of prayer ever since.
Monasteries and convents soon arose for the
Dominicans, and a Third Order.

THE EDUCATION OF CHIVALRY.—While most
men were getting their education in monasteries,
little schools in the cities were also growing up.

Sometimes money was left to support a priest, who was supposed to say Mass for the soul of his benefactor and teach the local children in the rest of his time. Sometimes guilds of craftsmen, or wealthy citizens, would employ a priest to teach their fellows.

Quite another sort of education took place in the houses of the great nobles and knights—this was the School of Chivalry. Till he was seven or eight a knight's son learned from his mother his prayers, his manners, and a healthy way of living. He then became a page in his own house, or that of a nobler knight than his father. There he learnt to do small services for his master and mistress, play the harp or pipe, run, wrestle, box; he also learned Latin from the house-priest, how to read and write, and make verses. At fourteen he was a squire, waited at table, hunted with his mistress, kept his master's horse and arms in condition, and became skilled in knightly warfare. At twenty-one, after fasting and prayer, the squire entered a church in full armour, and spent the night in prayer. In the early morning he made his confession, received Holy Communion, presented his sword to be blessed by the priest, and swore " TO DEFEND THE CHURCH, TO ATTACK THE WICKED, TO RESPECT THE PRIESTHOOD, TO PROTECT WOMEN AND THE POOR, TO PRESERVE THE COUNTRY IN PEACE, AND TO SHED HIS BLOOD IF

NEED BE FOR HIS BRETHREN." His overlord then laid his own sword on his shoulder (the accolade), and said, " In the Name of God, of Our Lady, of thy patron saint and of St Michael and St George, I dub thee Knight. Be bold, brave, and loyal."

All knights did not keep their great vow, nor interpret it well. They could be cruel, wastefully extravagant, discourteous to women of low rank, and despise their peasants. But there were some who tried to live up to their ideal, and the important thing to remember is that the knightly ideal expressed the essential teaching of the Christian Church, that the strong should help the weak. St Louis, king of France, was among the greatest of true Christian knights.

CHAPTER XII

THE WITNESS OF NOBLE MEN
THIRTEENTH CENTURY
ST LOUIS OF FRANCE, 1214-1270

KING LOUIS of France must have had a training
in chivalry much the same as this, though his
mother saw to it that he had more teaching from
priests and scholars than an ordinary knight's son,
and the vow of knighthood must have meant
much to him. He had been brought up to love
and honour the Church. He heard his Mass and
said his Hours all the time when he was travelling about with the Queen Regent in the dark,
dangerous days of his childhood, when the great
French nobles were trying to wrest the power into
their own hands. He kept his rules of prayer all
his life afterwards. He would go out to his early
worship daily and come back quietly so as not to
disturb the knights who slept in his room. He
would say his Hours with his priest as he rode out
on horseback, or hear them read when he was too
ill to speak himself.

The early part of the King's life was spent in
keeping peace with his neighbours and establishing

peace in France. It was a turbulent time, but
he kept a level head. He protested against the
Pope's action in deposing the Emperor Frederick,
a thing Louis thought he had no right to do; but
when Frederick captured some French bishops
who were summoned to a Papal council, he sent
him so stern a message that the prisoners were
released at his demand. He helped to finance the
Crusades, and guarded the Crusaders' castles in
their absence; he used his power to help to
suppress the Albigensians, but he did his best to
rescue innocent persons from false accusations.
He would not let the French Jews lend money at
a high rate of interest, and made them give back
their wrongful gains, but he would not persecute
them as some kings did. He succeeded in establishing his power in France, and made a truce
with England.

In 1248, in gratitude to God for his recovery
from an illness, the King sailed out to fight the
Sultan of Egypt who had conquered Jerusalem,
stopping at Cyprus on the way, where he was able
to settle a quarrel between the Templars and
Hospitallers, and make peace between the Catholic
and Orthodox Churches there. De Joinville, the
King's fine seneschal, has written the story of
Louis' heroic battles, of his capture and loss of
Damietta. He tells how he protected the wives
and children of his defeated foes, kept brave and

cheerful under horrible conditions of famine and disease, burying dead Christians with his own hands ; how he refused to desert his people in time of danger, kept faith with his enemies even when they broke faith with him, and calmly faced torture and death at their hands. They let him go for a ransom, and even then he stayed on in Palestine, hoping to do some good there. But the Crusade was a terrible failure, and it was a saddened King who came back to his welcoming country leaving so great a part of his fine army dead of wounds and disease.

From this time onward he gave himself more earnestly than ever to the service of God and his country.

In the first part of his reign Louis had obtained for France two most holy relics—a crown of thorns believed to be that worn by Our Lord, and a piece of the true Cross. Bareheaded and barefooted for reverence, amid the light of myriads of candles and the ringing of church bells, the royal family had borne these holy things to a place of honour, and Louis had built the Holy Chapel (Sainte Chapelle) to house them, a shrine of wonderful beauty which is still one of the loveliest things in Europe. In these times three great cathedrals were building, at Amiens and Rheims and Beauvais. New colleges sprang up at the Paris University under the King's patronage, for

D*

he loved and respected learning. He had copies
of the Scriptures, and the Christian writings of early
times, made for his own library, and felt honoured
when two famous scholars, Robert of the Sor-
bonne and Thomas Aquinas, dined at his table.

From that table every day the King had a
hundred poor people fed, serving some of them
with his own hands. His gifts and his kindness
went out to hospitals and almshouses and monasteries, to poor gentlefolk and widows and old,
disabled men who could no longer work. To
meet these expenses he cut down his own, ate
simple food, and used simple clothes and horse-
trappings, except where royal dignity and hospitality demanded splendour.

But the King's greatest work was the establish-
ment of justice. Twice a week it was his custom
to go out and sit under an oak in the wood of
Vincennes, and there rich and poor brought their
quarrels to him and he gave judgment. De
Joinville has pictured him there, in his tunic of
camlet and sleeveless surcoat and black mantle of
taffetas, and his hat with its white peacocks' feathers.
He forbade the nobles to make private war on
each other, or to settle their affairs by duels (where
the richest man could often hire the best fighter),
and it was during his reign that the Court of the
Barons came to be a real Parliament where law
was administered justly. Rich and powerful men

could not buy themselves off punishment, and the poor got a hearing. De Joinville, Godfrey of Beaulieu, his confessor, and William of Chartres, his almoner, have told us stories of the King's private life, his fasts and penances and scourgings and wearing of a hair shirt, and other stories of his kindness and courtesy and laughter and love of good talk. His seneschal adored him, though he blames him for having a hot temper, and for saying his prayers when he should have been looking after his wife ! And Godfrey of Beaulieu writes : " There was something in the mere sight of him that found a way to the hearts and affections of all."

The King had never forgotten his Crusade, and in 1270, though he was ill and unfit to travel, much less to fight, he set out again for the Holy Land, against the advice of his best counsellors. He only reached Africa, and there the fever which had killed so many of his comrades struck him down. He passed away peacefully, his arms crossed, smiling. Never had the knight's vow been more honourably kept.

" There was peace in his time," wrote a historian not long after his death ; " He loved God and Holy Church ; and they say he is with the saints."

NOTES   .   .   .   .

THE UNIVERSITIES AND THE SCHOOLMEN.—The end of the twelfth century saw the rise of the universities, originally guilds of teachers who united for help and protection. Though most of these teachers had been taught and employed by the Church, they were not now all monks or clerics. They attracted students from all countries, some of whom became great teachers themselves. Such was PETER ABELARD (*d.* 1142), the young Breton student at Paris, whose brilliant wit and daring thought attracted to his lectures students by the hundred. Abelard believed that the apparent contradictions in the works of the old Christian writers should be studied and discussed to arrive at the truth, and for this purpose he wrote a book called *Yes and No*, which stated one hundred and fifty-eight debatable subjects, and left the student to find the truth as best he could. Good Church people of the time were shocked by the book, and St Bernard finally got Abelard silenced. But the method of stating the arguments for and against became the chief way of teaching in the universities.

Universities sprang up at Salermo, where medicine was the chief subject; Paris, which was chiefly theological; Bologna, where law was specially studied; and then in England, France,

Italy, Spain, and later in Germany. Popes and kings granted them charters to protect them and free them from taxation; they had their own governments and courts of law, and became exceedingly powerful. The students were organised in national groups or colleges, and in time the friars had their own colleges in the universities. The great teachers of these times were fascinated by the logic and learning of the old Greek writer ARISTOTLE (384-322 B.C.), whose writings were beginning to reach them through their contact with the Greek Empire and the Moors during the Crusades. They translated and explained his works, and harmonised his ideas with Church teaching. They loved logic above all other subjects, and did a great service to their fellows by training them in exact and detailed thinking. Unfortunately, as time went on, their teaching became dry and fussy, with the same emphasis on unimportant as on important things. The *Schoolmen*, as these teachers came to be called, taught none of the famous old literature of Greece and Rome, nor any history, and they despised the " modern " languages of their day. They trained men to think, but not to feel, and they did not set out to teach them to live rightly as the early monks had done. So it is not surprising that many of the students, poor and wandering men, badly housed and fed in the great overcrowded cities to which they came, ended by being tramps, thieves, and drunkards, for all their learning. On the other hand, just because the universities were free, and could discuss and explore everything, they made learning available to everyone, and greatly increased the world's store of knowledge.

The first of the schoolmen to be influenced by the method and writings of Aristotle was ANSELM (1033-1098), afterwards Archbishop of Canterbury. ALEXANDER HALES, an Englishman (*d.* 1245), was a teacher at Paris; JOACHIM, ABBOT of FLORIS, and JOHN of SALISBURY, were famed for their Biblical and literary studies; PETER LOMBARD (1100-1160) wrote a theological textbook for students called *The Sentences*; BONAVENTURA (1221-1274), DUNS SCOTUS (1275-1338), and WILLIAM of OCCAM (1280-1338), were famous Franciscans; so also was ROGER BACON (1214-1294), who was one of the first to base knowledge directly on observation. Two of the greatest of the schoolmen were of the Dominican Order, ALBERTUS MAGNUS and THOMAS AQUINAS.

CHAPTER XIII

THE ORGANISATION OF LEARNING
Thirteenth Century
THOMAS AQUINAS, 1225-1274

Thomas Aquinas was the son of noble parents, and connected with most of the reigning houses in Europe, including England. Born in the castle of Rocca Sicca, near Aquine, in South Italy, he had been sent to school with the Benedictines at Monte Cassino when he was five years old. He was a quiet, serious little boy, who had loved books as playthings even when a baby, and he startled the monks of Monte Cassino by asking them at once, " What is God ? "

Thomas spent the rest of his life answering that question, and others like it. He went to the University of Naples at ten (boys went to the universities as young as that in those days), and there he came across the Dominican Friars, and made up his mind to become one of them. His family was furious ; they could not bear to think of so noble a scholar becoming one of the begging friars, and his soldier brothers were sent to kidnap him and carry him off, which they did. He was imprisoned at Rocca Sicca, but nothing would alter his mind. Finally, his brothers relented, and let him down from his prison window in a basket, where some waiting friars took him back to the monastery with them. But it was only after an interview with the Pope that the matter was finally settled. Thomas was then sent to Cologne to study there under the famous Albertus Magnus. The students thought his quiet manner dull, and believed him to be stupid, so they called him Dumb Ox. But the time came when he was given a thesis to defend in public, and then he startled everyone, including his master. In his calm, precise manner he stated every objection against his own case and answered each of them, then proposed his own solution and settled the matter. Albertus tried to puzzle him with some difficult questions, but his student answered them all. Then he cried out in amazement, " We call this young man Dumb Ox, but so loud will be his bellowing that it will resound throughout the whole world." The prophecy came true. Thomas went back with his master to found a Dominican school at Cologne, took his Master's Degree in Paris in 1256, became a popular preacher, was called to Rome by the Pope in 1261, and to professorships in Bologna, Paris, and Naples in turn, as one of the greatest scholars of his time. As a Dominican Friar he travelled far to attend the General Chapter of his Order, wherever it was held, and in 1263 he visited the Dominican Priory in Holborn in London.

His work was especially that of organising the teaching of students, and writing books on the Christian faith, which are still famous throughout the world. It was an age for collecting, classifying and summarising the wisdom of past writers. There were many books, but the knowledge they contained seemed to many students (as it had to Peter Abelard), confused, untidy, indecisive, " Yes and No." Thomas Aquinas, with his splendid memory, his endless patience, his subtle, logical mind, his untiring energy, and his steady faith, was the man to summarise the Faith, and he spent his life doing it.

Among the many books that he wrote, on the Scriptures, Theology, Astrology, Psychology, Philosophy, and Civil Government, the two most famous are *The Sum of Theology* and *The Truth of the Catholic Faith against the Gentiles*. He wrote the last for those who were teaching the Jewish and Moorish converts in Spain, and in it he dealt with nearly all the questions that anyone can ask about God and His creatures. He also wrote an Office (hymns, prayers and selected Scripture readings) for a new Festival to honour the

Institution of the Holy Eucharist,[1] and his prayers and hymns are used by half of Christendom to-day.

Those who lived with Aquinas have given us a very clear picture of him—a big, fair man, quiet and courteous in his manner, and without a trace of vanity. He was gentle and considerate with his students, very methodical in his work, and, like many great scholars, very absent-minded. Once, as he dined at the royal palace, he went off into deep thought, and suddenly struck the table, crying, " That finishes the Manichean heresy." The worried Prior pulled his cape : " Remember, my master, that you are at the table with the King of France." Aquinas bowed to the King and begged his pardon. But he went on being absent-minded at meals.

Whilst Aquinas taught those truths which he believed God had revealed to the Christian Church, and those truths which men's minds can discover by logical argument, he also knew that nothing he could say could wholly explain the greatness of God. Sometimes in his prayers he saw and felt what was too wonderful and mysterious to be described at all. " It must be respected by silence," he would say to those who asked him what he had seen. It was after one of such

[1] Which was called the Feast of Corpus Christi (the Body of Christ).

prayers, towards the end of his life, that he said. " Such things have been revealed to me that all I have written seems to me of small account."

In 1274 he was called to a Council by the Pope, and he left Naples at the command. But he only reached the Cistercian monastery at Fossa Nuova, and there the illness that had been growing on him became worse, and he could go no farther. They brought him the Sacrament, which he welcomed with joy and reverence, the great words of the Te Deum on his lips, " Thou art the King of Glory, O Christ, Thou art the everlasting Son of the Father." Before morning he had passed away.

NOTES . . . .

MONKS AND CLERGY IN THE THIRTEENTH CENTURY.—While Thomas Aquinas was teaching in Cologne in 1248, Eudes Rigaud, Archbishop of Rouen, visited the cathedrals and convents of his diocese, and has left us a record of what he found. He tells of ignorant clergy and their clerks, who drank and swore and cheated, and even killed men in tavern brawls ; and of nuns who did not keep their rules of silence, had pet animals, and kept boxes full of private possessions.

This account is typical of the ignorance and bad discipline which prevailed in many monasteries and parishes. Bishops and priests who outwardly accepted the rule which forbade them to marry, often had wives and children all the same. Many bishops lived with their clergy in community under a Rule, and were called *Augustinian Canons*, but the Rule was very rarely kept. The Benedictines had become rich through their hard work and plain living and the gifts showered upon them, and though they still did much to help the poor and build churches and monasteries, their wealth had made some of them luxurious and lazy, according to a monk's standard. Moreover, there were many people in convents who had no business to be there, sons and daughters whose parents wished to get them out of the way, but who had never been called by God to this sort of life, men kept there for fear of their enemies, and people whom nobody wanted elsewhere. These did great harm to monastic life. On the other hand, there were good men like Rigaud, who tried to reform the clergy, and good monks like those of Citeaux, who kept the old strict way of living, and noble women like SAINT ELIZABETH of HUNGARY, who belonged to the Third Order of St Francis, and really lived in the spirit of its founder. And there were all those unnamed men and women who lived truly Christian lives and who, by their gifts and their labour, helped to build and to make beautiful those glorious churches and abbeys which are still the greatest treasures of Christendom, and in which Christian worship has never ceased.

CHAPTER XIV

THE WORSHIP OF THE MIDDLE AGES

Thirteenth and Fourteenth Centuries

Mediæval Churches and Craftsmen

In the days of St Francis, St Louis, and St Thomas Aquinas, and in the century that followed, a great change took place in the building of churches in Western Christendom. Instead of the solid, round-arched Norman churches, taller, lighter buildings began to be constructed, with thin walls and vaulted roofs supported from the outside by buttresses. The arches were pointed, stone ribs sprang from the walls and pillars; the stone was carved into foliage and fruit and flowers and birds and animals, stone statues of great beauty and dignity were set in niches, and everything glowed with colour—scarlet and emerald and azure and gold. Where the wall-spaces were not lit by immense windows of coloured glass, they were painted with pictures or hung with bright woven tapestries; and in the choir, wooden seats, marvellously carved, were set up. The people of those days believed that God loved and was honoured by beauty, and they put as much work into those things which He alone could see as into that which all could gaze on.

From the high church towers great bells called the people to worship, and when the bells ceased there was the sound of that old and lovely music which had been sung, with little variation, for close on a thousand years.

The supreme act of worship in the Middle Ages was the Mass. The lines of every church building led up to and centred on the altar, and there all the most precious of the craftsman's work was gathered together. The chalice might be silver or gold, set with precious stones, or emblazoned with glowing enamel by the workmen of Limoges, the priests' garments and the altar frontal worked in silk and gold thread by the skilled embroideresses of England, and the Mass book written and decorated so as to be a joy and a wonder to all that saw it.

As the people believed that Our Lord was present in a very special and important way in this service, so also they believed that the prayer offered at Mass was more powerful than other prayers, and for this reason they reverenced their priests, who alone could say Mass. People left money in their wills to support priests who would say Masses[1] for their souls after they were dead,

[1] See p. 114.

in the little chapels (or chantries) in which their tombs were placed. Whenever they wanted to pray for something important, or give thanks, they had a Mass said for that purpose. Sermons were preached at Mass, though not always ; but Bible stories and tales from the lives of the saints were always before the eyes of worshippers in the windows or on the walls, and were represented at special seasons in miracle plays. People learnt by seeing rather than by hearing ; they knew what the priest was doing, even when they could not always hear his voice nor understand the Latin words he spoke. A few of the richer and better educated people had books of prayers written in their own language.

The churches, cathedrals and abbeys of these times were originated, and sometimes designed, by famous bishops and abbots. Suger, the Abbot of St Denis, in St Bernard's days, first began to use the new style of architecture which has been described. But the actual work, and sometimes the designing, was done by the master-masons and their craftsmen. We know many of the French master-masons' names, though few of the English ; Pierre de Mountereau built a part of St Denis and Notre Dame at Paris, and perhaps the lovely shrine of St Chapelle. Among the painters of churches there was Giotto, the son of a peasant landowner, who made pictures from

the life of St Francis for the church at Assisi,
and besides his other famous paintings, designed
the cathedral at Florence. Before the fourteenth
century was over, Fra Angelico was born, the
gentle Dominican monk whose work became so
famous that the Pope sent for him to paint frescoes
and illuminate books at Rome. These were the
first of that line of Italian painters whose master-
pieces were inspired by the Faith they professed,
and are known all over the civilised world.
Sometimes a craftsman would put his name in an
illuminated book, or on a bell, but for the most
part the men who made the marvellous beauty
of these churches are not known to us by name.

The worship of God went on all through the
day and night. The monks said their Hours in
the monasteries, and there were men and women
who lived alone in one or two tiny cells adjoining
a church and gave their whole lives to the work
of prayer and praise. They were called Anchorets,
and Anchoresses, and the most well-known of
English anchoresses was Juliana of Norwich, who
wrote a famous book on the love of God. Hermits
gave their lives to prayer and praise too, though
they were free to go about from place to place.
Such were Guthlac of the Fens in the seventh
century, and Godric of Weardale in the twelfth,
and Richard Rolle of Hampole in these times.
The mediæval Church honoured many kinds of

Christian people, but it reverenced most deeply those whom it called Contemplatives, whose life was spent in meditation on God and adoration of Him.

NOTES   .   .   .   .

WRONG IDEAS AND PRACTICES.—Just as there were great saints and exceedingly bad men in this period, so the beauty of its worship was often spoiled by ignorance, foolish superstitions, and the wrong use of good things.

The Catholic Church had always taught that the bread and wine through which Our Lord gives Himself to His worshippers must be treated with reverence. The Schoolmen had worked out a theory in terms of the philosophy of their own times to explain exactly how He comes to us in this way. This theory, called *Transubstantiation*, was a very high spiritual doctrine, but it was difficult to understand and explain, and when ignorant priests taught it, their listeners often got the idea that the Holy Bread must be worshipped like an idol and used like a charm. People sometimes stole it to use for themselves. Thus a good deal of irreverence and superstition crept into the worship at Mass.

So also it was taught that Holy Communion must be received with great reverence, and that people must confess their sins and intend to lead a good life before they communicated. But many people would not do this, and got into the habit of simply hearing Mass instead, and so received the Holy Sacrament very rarely indeed.

The Catholic Church had also taught that the saints and martyrs, because of their goodness, should be honoured after their death. People were encouraged to put up statues to their memory, to venerate anything that belonged to them, and to ask them to pray for them. The shrines where their relics lay were enriched by gorgeous gifts and were the goals of great pilgrimages. (One of the richest and most famous places of pilgrimage was the shrine of Thomas à Becket in Canterbury.) From very early times, especially from the fifth century, Christians had honoured the Mother of Christ in this way, above all other saints, and some of their noblest churches had been built in her honour and called by her name. But the Church also taught that while saints were to be honoured, God alone must be worshipped. Unfortunately the common people often paid far more attention to the saints than to God. They felt that the saints, and especially Our Lady, would be more lenient to their sins, and would persuade God to give them what they dare not ask for themselves. So a very wrong attitude towards God began to grow up.

The Catholic Church had also taught that all Christian people, alive or dead, are part of one great fellowship, and that prayer helps those who have died just as much as it did when they were on earth. But around this idea there grew up some bad customs; it was held that some particular prayer, or some good deed, or so much money given to a church, would help the dead exactly so much, and God's own power and mercy were sometimes forgotten.

All this was due to bad teaching, or not enough teaching, and also to the fact that in these days ordinary people rarely read or heard the Bible in their own language.

POPES AND KINGS.—Christian people were not only troubled by these things, but also by the continual quarrelling between the popes and the rulers of Europe. The Papacy had never seemed so powerful as in the jubilee year of 1300 when pilgrims poured into Rome by thousands, bringing their gifts. Yet only three years later the Pope died through the insults and ill-treatment of the French King's army, and from 1305-1377 the popes were compelled to live at Avignon in order to be under the influence of France.[1] They lived luxuriously and increased their taxation in all countries, and this met with opposition, especially in England, where the French were regarded as enemies.

---

[1] This came to be called " The Babylonish Captivity."

SOME REFORMERS.—Men and women in the fourteenth century tried to reform the Church in three ways :

Some began by trying to live a strictly good and self-sacrificing life themselves, influencing others as far as they could by word and example. Such were the Brethren of the Common Lot in Flanders, a community who shared their goods and gave themselves to prayer and study and good works. THOMAS À KEMPIS, who wrote one of the most famous of all Christian books, *The Imitation of Christ*, once belonged to them, though he afterwards became a monk. Such, too, was ST CATHERINE OF SIENA (*d.* 1380), whose noble life and teaching not only influenced many persons, but helped to bring the Pope back to his duty at Rome.

A second party attacked the evils of the time openly, many of them setting forth new theories of the claims of Church and State, and limiting or denying the power of the Pope. Among these were WILLIAM of OCCAM, MARSILIUS of PADUA,[1] (1270-1336), DANTE (1265-1321), and JOHN WYCLIF (1324-84), who also sent out his Poor Preachers (LOLLARDS) to read the Bible to the English in their own tongue. In Bohemia there were also

[1] Who first asserted that the Catholic faith rests on Scripture only, and that all difficult questions should be settled by a General Council in which both clergy and laity are present.

CONRAD of WALDHAUSEN, JOHN HUS (1369-1415), and JEROME of PRAGUE. These two last fell into the power of the Papal party and were burned as heretics. They were good men and heroes to their own people, and their deaths increased the anger of the Bohemians against the Pope and the clergy.

There was also a third party of reformers who denounced the evils of their times openly, but remained loyal to the Pope and to the Church system of government. Such was the author of *Piers Plowman*.

In the fifteenth century the evils in Church and State increased. There was more opposition to the Papacy, and the reformers gained more power. Things were made at once better and worse by what is known as the RENAISSANCE, or REVIVAL of LEARNING, one of whose most famous scholars was ERASMUS.

CHAPTER XV

THE NEW LEARNING
Fifteenth and Sixteenth Centuries
DESIDERIUS ERASMUS, 1466–1536

DESIDERIUS ERASMUS was born into a world where tremendous changes were taking place. The idea of a single Western Empire under Pope and Emperor was fading, and nations with their rulers were asserting their independence. Many of the activities which had once been organised and directly governed by the Church were passing into the hands of lay people. The universities and schools were getting new ideas about education and putting them into practice. Individuals were beginning to feel their independence too, and to dare to criticise the evils that they saw around them as they had never done before, and this was further stimulated by the invention of printing, which made it possible for people to get at more books and study and discuss things privately with greater freedom.

Great new discoveries were being made in the Western world by the Portuguese explorers, and great new discoveries were being made by scholars in the world of literature. For some centuries the writings of the ancient Greeks and Romans had been neglected or lost ; now men were recovering them, and the vision of the wonderful civilisation of that ancient world was overwhelming. The break-up of the Eastern Empire, and the sack of Constantinople in 1453, had sent Greek scholars westward, and Europe went mad over the Greek language.

It was a restless, excited, adventurous age.

The new spirit first awoke in Italy, and put new life into education and art ; though many men, in their worship of the old pagan literature, became pagan in their ideas and morals, whilst they kept the Christian name, and this was very bad for the Church. But north of the Alps men were interested in the New Learning, not only for its own sake, but because it helped them to read and understand the writings of the early Christians and to get at the New Testament in the language in which it was originally written. They felt that many of the ideas and practices of the Catholic Church were not Christian, and they wanted to know how the early Church taught and practised the Faith.

Erasmus was a Dutchman, born at Rotterdam. He had been an Augustinian canon and a priest, but he was released from his monastic vows by the Pope, and travelled about Europe, lecturing, translating, and writing for the rest of his life. He studied in Paris, and then came to England with one of his pupils, Lord Mountjoy. Here he made friends with all the great Englishmen of the time who loved the New Learning—Warham, Archbishop of Canterbury ; the two teachers of Greek, Grocyn and Linacre; John Colet, who lectured on St Paul's Epistles and founded a famous school ; and that wise and witty lawyer, Sir Thomas More. After two years Erasmus went back to the Continent, and visited France and Italy and Belgium and Switzerland, coming back to England again, and finally settling down to end his days in the city of Basle.

All his life Erasmus sought after two ideals, Truth and Peace. He was always trying to get at the best and purest manuscripts, editing and translating them, and pointing out to people what the writers had really said and meant. He edited and published a New Testament in Greek, after having compared the oldest and best manuscripts he could find, and he then translated it into Latin for the people who knew no Greek. It seemed dreadful to him that so many people who honoured pictures and statues of Jesus Christ should never have read for themselves the story of His life. " Statues . . . only profess to represent to us the outer form of His body," he wrote, " while these books present us with a living picture of His

5

holy mind." In the same way he edited or translated the writings of the Fathers of the Church,
Origen and Jerome and Chrysostom, and many
more.

Erasmus also served truth by making people
laugh at the shams and silliness and dark cruel
ignorance of his times, but he made them laugh
in such a way that they saw the serious meaning
behind his jokes. In his famous book *The Praise
of Folly*, he laughed at the wealth and worldly
power of the popes and the dull, fussy teaching
of the schoolmen, at lazy ignorant monks and
nuns, at people who treated the statues of the
saints as gods, and at those who thought that by
giving so much money to a church they could
escape the consequences of their sins. He
laughed, too, at the scholars who went mad over
the New Learning and could think of nothing
else, and he laughed at some of the Germans who
wanted to reform the Church and were so impressed with their own ideas that they talked " as
if there had been no Gospel for thirteen hundred
years ! "

Erasmus wrote also in the service of Peace.
He tried to make princes see how wicked and
cruel were the wars into which they led their
people, and in this he was far ahead of the thinkers
of his day. He also hated the quarrel which
was beginning to rage so furiously between the

authorities of the Catholic Church and those who wanted to reform it. Erasmus did not want to sweep away the whole system of Church government and Church practices, only to purify them, and he refused to take sides in the matter. "I will not and I can not serve a party," he wrote; "I would that all might strive together for the triumph of Christ and the peace of the Gospel, and that without violence, but in truth and reason, we might take counsel together for the dignity of the priesthood and for the liberty of the people whom Our Lord Jesus Christ desired to be free."

There is a portrait of Erasmus, done by one of the world's most famous artists, and it tells us a great deal about him. It shows a sad, clever, sensitive, sharp-nosed face, with a little twinkle of laughter hidden in it. You are not at all sure what he is thinking, and it is not surprising that the people of his own time could not understand Erasmus. The Church authorities sometimes suspected that he was not a good Catholic, and the reformers thought he really belonged to them but was too cowardly to say so. Erasmus was not a perfect hero, either. He grumbled aloud about everything, he begged for money from his friends, he was afraid of suffering, and came very near telling lies to avoid it, though he was at least honest and brave enough to own that he was a coward. But he was a hero nevertheless, for he strove for truth in the Church, and he spent his life trying to make men face the facts and see all sides of the questions that troubled them, and that is one of the hardest things in the world.

NOTES . . . .

COLLEGES AND COLLEGIATE CHURCHES.—At the end of the fourteenth century William of Wykeham had founded his two schools, or colleges, for poor scholars at Oxford (1386) and Winchester (1393). These schools were meant to give the scholars not only free education, but religious teaching and a disciplined life, such as the universities could not provide. From this time many new (and now famous) colleges were founded, and hospitals and almshouses for the poor were built, each with a fine church attached to it. Many of these great " collegiate " churches can still be seen in England. These were the " charities " of the time, as monasteries had once been. But the monasteries were declining, fewer people entered them, and sometimes it was agreed to suppress the smallest of them in order to found colleges and almshouses.

The church architecture of the time was greatly influenced by the Renaissance, and there was a return to the style of the old pagan temples of

Greece and Rome.[1] In England the style of church building which came into being at this time is called PERPENDICULAR, because most of its lines ran straight up and down or across, instead of being curved.

THE REIGN OF HENRY VIII.—A year before Erasmus died news was brought to him of the death of his friend Sir Thomas More, one among many of the brave Catholics who laid down their lives rather than submit to their immoral and tyrannical King. Henry had abolished the Papal power in England and established the Royal Supremacy because he was determined to do whatever he wished without anyone hindering him. He did not want either the supporters of the Pope or the followers of Luther to gain power in England, so he beheaded Catholics if they would not recognise him as head of the Church, and burned Protestants as heretics if they denied the doctrine of transubstantiation. He was able to carry out his plans for two reasons ; firstly, because England had always been independent in spirit and had often objected to various papal claims and exactions ; and secondly, because the Church of his days was weakened by the evils Erasmus had condemned, the discontent of the reformers, and the greed of those who were ready to support

[1] Pope Julius II began to rebuild the great church of St Peter at Rome in this style.

any arrangement that would bring them more money.

Within a few years the King had extorted great sums of money from the clergy and suppressed the monasteries and chantries, seizing their wealth mainly for himself and his courtiers. His weak Archbishop, THOMAS CRANMER, approved all his actions and obeyed his commands; his brutal minister, THOMAS CROMWELL, sent innumerable men and women to the block and the stake. The clergy seemed utterly powerless to resist the King. The common people rose in a rebellion (*The Pilgrimage of Grace*), but they dispersed, trusting promises which were never fulfilled. Kings had had great power in the English Church before this, but there had always been another court of appeal; now everything depended on the will of the King alone.

Two good things emerged from this reign of terror. An English Bible was set up in every church and ordered to be read at the Church services, and the splendid English Litany, made by Cranmer largely from old Latin sources, was ordered to be used.

INDULGENCES.—We saw that the revolt against those in authority in the Church had a good deal to do with money, and it was the Pope's attempt to get money for his new church buildings at this time, which brought about the second great break in Christendom. The quarrel arose over the sale of *Indulgences*. An Indulgence was a " let-off " punishment. Catholics believed that all wrong-doing was punished, either in this life or in that state after death (called Purgatory) in which the soul is made ready for the perfect happiness of Heaven. It was held that great saints probably went straight to Heaven, but that most ordinary people would have to spend some time in Purgatory enduring their punishment. The Pope was held to have the power to shorten the time spent in Purgatory by granting Indulgences to people, either for themselves or for their dead friends. These Indulgences were to be sold on condition that those who bought them were really sorry for their sins and intended to lead a good life, and the very poor were not asked to pay anything for them. Nevertheless, the sale of Indulgences had a very bad effect. The agents who sold them tried to get as much money as possible out of them, and those who bought them often felt as if they had cleared off one lot of sins and could begin on another. The dreadful thing about the whole business was that it encouraged people only to think of getting rid of punishment, and to forget that their sins hurt God and shamed the Church. Serious Catholics preached against these evils. In Italy a fine preaching friar, BERNARDINE of SIENA, publicly denounced the methods of the Indulgence-sellers. In Germany, in the year 1517, a monk and Doctor of Theology named MARTIN LUTHER, nailed up ninety-five theses to the church door in Wittenberg, as the custom was, to tell those who were interested that he would hold a disputation on the subject.

CHAPTER XVI

THE PROTESTANTS
Sixteenth Century
MARTIN LUTHER, 1483–1546

WHEN Martin Luther nailed up his theses, written in Latin, he hoped that someone would come forward and debate with him, but no one came. Instead, the theses were translated into German and printed, and within a fortnight nearly all Germany was talking of them.

What Luther said was this : Indulgences are not important because they do not help people to be good ; when people are really sorry for their sins they do not try to escape punishment ; it is far better to give money to the poor than to buy Indulgences, for kindness makes us good, but Indulgences only free us from punishment. Besides, said Luther, it is very difficult for us preachers to defend the Pope when the Indulgence-sellers talk as they do. These words sank deep into people's minds, and from that time the sale of Indulgences began to decline.

Then Luther's opponents began to defend their position, and Luther wrote his own defence to

the Pope. He was summoned to Rome, but he
claimed the right to be heard in his own country,
and was allowed to meet the Papal Legate on
German soil, but no agreement could be reached.
Luther then wrote an appeal for a General
Council to set things right, and he published
the three great creeds of the Church in German,
so that everyone could see what were the
central and essential beliefs of the Catholic
Church. Up to this time Luther had believed
in the Church government that existed in his
day, but when he came to debate with Dr
Eck, the Catholic theologian, at Leipsic (1518),
he realised that he did not believe in the
supreme power of the Papacy, and from that
time onward he appealed to the German people,
in burning language, to take matters into their
own hands.

What Luther wanted was a German national
Church with its own council acting independently,
and much greater freedom in many matters. He
thought, for instance, that men and women
should become monks and nuns if they wished,
but should leave their convents if they found that
this was not the right life for them, and that
priests should be allowed to marry. He thought
that there were too many Church festivals on
which people were forbidden to work, too many
begging friars for the towns to support, and too

many pilgrimages which encouraged begging and superstition.

Luther insisted that the salvation of men came from their faith in God Who alone had power to save them, and not from their own good works. This is called the doctrine of *Justification by Faith*. He held that men's prayers and good works ought to spring out of love and gratitude to God, Whose loving-kindness they can never repay, and not be treated as a sort of spiritual banking account.

He also taught that monks and nuns do not live a higher or better life than those who serve God in their daily work in the world, and he believed that priests were ordinary men chosen to represent the people whose worship they conducted, not persons to whom the Church had given a power and character which could never be taken away.

The Pope excommunicated Luther, and ordered his writings to be burned. Luther publicly burned the Book of Church (Canon) Law, and his students, in wild excitement, burnt the Pope's Bull and Dr Eck's books in a great bonfire at Wittenberg.

Just then the seven princes who had the right to elect the Emperor, chose Charles V to be their ruler, and Luther was summoned before him and the National Assembly (Diet) at Worms to state his beliefs. He set out with some friends in a covered cart, the Imperial Herald riding before them, his yellow banner with its double eagle showing that they were under the Emperor's protection. He preached wherever he stopped on the way, and the crowds were wild with enthusiasm. People rushed from their houses to see him as he entered the city, and while the Diet sat, threats were written up on the walls to say that there would be an armed rising if he were harmed. Standing before the Emperor on the second day of his appearance, Luther stated plainly that he could not be bound by the statements of either the Pope or General Councils, but that he could only act by his conscience and the teaching of the Scriptures. "I can do nothing else; here I stand, so help me God," he said.

Luther went back to his lodgings. Charles V wanted the Pope's favour just then, so he dismissed the German princes who were friendly to Luther, as if all was over; and then, calling the rest together, he proclaimed Luther to be an outlaw twenty days after he had left the city.

But Luther's friends were prepared. His cart had travelled just over a week when it was stopped by a band of horsemen who dashed out of a thick wood and seized and carried him off with them. In the great castle of the Wartburg the Elector of Saxony hid and protected him ; he was dressed as a poor knight and called George. From this hiding-place he wrote to his friends, and here he began to translate the New Testament into German. There had been other translations before this, but none were so vivid or understandable as the one Luther made. (Later, with the help of other scholars, he translated the Old Testament.)

In the meantime Germany was in a terrible state of confusion. The Emperor was mostly away in his other dominions, and each great noble was nearly supreme in his own district ; but there was great discontent among the poorer knights and among the down-trodden peasants. People supported Luther from very different reasons. Some did so because they hated the Pope's taxes and wanted a free and united Germany ; others, like the peasants, thought that his talk about Christian liberty meant that they ought to be free from their burden of bondage. Some wanted to destroy everything that belonged to the old order of things, and at Wittenberg the University was closed, the Church services ceased, and the monks and nuns were persecuted.

Luther was in a terribly difficult position. He did not want to destroy all the old customs, nor to force his teaching on unwilling people, and, on the other hand, he was very much afraid that, if there was a social revolution, people would say it was all his fault. His teaching would be condemned, and all that he had striven for would be lost. He left his hiding-place, and calmed the people of Wittenberg, so that after a little while things became normal again. He tried to stop the Peasant Rising, but when it really broke out, and they attacked castles and monasteries, he called on the nobles to kill them without mercy. Luther was bitterly ashamed of his cruel words afterwards, but the poorest of the people never trusted him again. In many parts of Germany Luther's ideas were put into practice, and he spent the rest of his life teaching and preaching and travelling about to organise the new Church life and education. He married Catherine von Bora, who had once been a nun, and they lived very happily with their children in what had been Luther's convent in Wittenberg. There he wrote his Catechisms, and hymns also, two of which are very well known and loved to-day—" *Away in a Manger*," and " *A safe stronghold*." When the plague came to Wittenberg, Luther bravely stayed among his people. He died peacefully in 1546, the hero of his nation.

NOTES . . . .

THE PROTESTANTS IN GERMANY.—The people who followed Luther's teaching came to be called *Protestants*, because a number of Lutheran princes *protested* against the Emperor trying to alter the decision of the Diet of Speyer (1526), which allowed each province to settle its own religious affairs. It was finally agreed at the Peace of Augsburg that the religion of each province should be that of its Prince, and those who disagreed with it must emigrate (1555). Lutheran churches were governed by councils, whose members were appointed by the chief civic authority of the district, for Luther did not believe that the ordinary people were fit to govern themselves ; and thus the princes came to have great power over the Church. These churches at first kept many of the old ways of worship—they had pictures and crucifixes as well as music, and observed the main Christian festivals, but they introduced a great deal of hymn-singing, and they made the sermon the most important part of the service.

The Protestants organised a number of elementary schools and high schools. Luther believed that the State ought to maintain and control the schools, and compel children to attend them, though he also believed that they ought to spend part of their time learning their own trade. The chief study in the schools was the Bible.

Other famous German reformers were CARL-STADT, ULRICH VON HUTTEN, PHILIP OF HESSE, MARTIN BUCER (1497-1560), who finally settled in England, and PHILIP MELANCHTHON, Luther's gentle student friend, who drew up the Augsburg Confession, which is a statement of the Lutheran faith.

THE PROTESTANTS IN SCANDINAVIA.—In Denmark and Sweden (to which Christianity had been brought by the heroic monk, ANSCAR OF CORBEY, in the ninth century) Protestantism became established partly through the convictions of the people, but mostly through the princes and nobles who wished to gain power by confiscating the great wealth of the Church. Later, however, the people became deeply attached to the beliefs that had been forced upon them.

THE REFORMED CHURCH IN SWITZERLAND.— The Church in Switzerland was reformed largely through one man, ULRICH ZWINGLI (1484-1531). It became independent (the Town Council nominating the pastors whom the people then elected) and abolished almost everything that could remind men of the " old religion," as it was called.

Zwingli did not believe that Our Lord is

present in any special way in the Eucharist, but thought of the service only as a memorial. Luther violently disagreed with him on this point, for he held the old belief, though he did not think it could be explained by the doctrine of Transubstantiation. Some of the Swiss Cantons became Catholic, others Protestant, and Zwingli was killed in a battle between the two parties.

THE PROTESTANT REVOLT, OR REFORMATION, had two great effects : on the one hand it forced everyone to face and try to set right many of the serious evils and abuses of good customs which had arisen in the Church, and it made them discuss and decide what they really believed about Church government and Church teaching. With the help of the Renaissance scholars it opened up the Bible to everyone, and the history of the early Church to scholars.

But it divided the Western Church so completely that before very long the two parties hopelessly misunderstood one another, each suspecting everything the other did, and refusing to have anything to do with each other's teaching and customs, however good they might be. It plunged Europe into religious wars which deepened the hatred and misunderstanding, and created a new wave of religious persecution.

In most of the Protestant countries the Church.

at first, was freed from the power of the Pope, only to be subjugated to the power of civil rulers, from whom there was no appeal. But after Luther's death there arose a man who created a system by which the Church asserted its supreme right. His name was JOHN CALVIN.

CHAPTER XVII
THE REFORMED CHURCH
SIXTEENTH CENTURY
JOHN CALVIN, 1509-1564

JOHN CALVIN (Jean Chauvin) was the son of a wealthy and educated French Catholic, who had first meant his son to be a priest, but afterwards had him trained as a lawyer. It was while he was studying law that Calvin met Peter Olivétan, a Protestant who was translating the Bible into French, and Melchior Wolmar, who was studying the New Testament in Greek ; and it was through these two men that he began to read the Bible for himself, and became convinced that the beliefs of the Protestants were right.

Calvin was a brilliant thinker and a born organiser, and in a very little while he became the leader of the Protestant community in Paris.

When persecution broke out he fled to Switzerland, but only in order to fight better for his cause, and put the Protestant case fairly before the King of France. Francis the First liked the Protestant scholars, but he was a Catholic, and very much influenced by his intolerant Queen

Mother and her counsellors, who told him that all Protestants were mad fanatics, determined to overthrow law and order. No written defence and explanation of the Reformed Faith existed until Calvin wrote his famous *Institutes of the Christian Religion* and sent the book to the King of France. This book was written in good Latin and translated into excellent French, and all who read it were impressed by the clear thinking and fine scholarship of its author.

In the year this book was published (1536), the city of Geneva had publicly established the Reformed Faith, with William Farel, a French Protestant, as its chief minister, and when Farel heard that Calvin was passing through the city, he searched him out and commanded him, in stern and urgent language, to stay on in the city and help with the work of reformation. Thus it was that Calvin came to Geneva, and began the great struggle of his life, to put into practice the beliefs he had stated, and to make Geneva a centre from which help and inspiration were to go out to his fellow Protestants in all parts of Europe.

The two great beliefs of Calvin's life were the tremendous greatness and majesty of God, and the necessity of a sober, righteous and godly life in those who were privileged to belong to the Christian Church.

All down the ages the Christian Church has

held two beliefs which seem to contradict each
other, but which are both necessary. The first
is, that God knows everything that will happen,
and wills or permits it to happen ; and the second
is, that our wills are free, and that we are responsible when we choose good or evil. Calvin put all
his emphasis on the first truth. But though he
preached that God has predestined everyone to a
good or evil end (*the Doctrine of Predestination*),
he also preached that no one but God knows that
end, and that therefore we should judge no one,
but each do his utmost to serve and obey God.
To help people to do that, Calvin thought that
the Church ought to appoint officials who were
to watch over the lives of all Christian people.

Calvin knew a great deal about the Church
of the first three centuries, and he thought he
was getting back to the earliest and best kind
of Church government when he organised the
Church at Geneva. There were four kinds of
officials in his church—preaching elders (or presbyters) who also administered the Sacraments ;
ruling elders (or presbyters) who were ordained
to help and govern the Church and watch over
the lives of the people ; teachers and deacons.
This system of government came to be called
PRESBYTERIAN. Calvin, like Luther, thought that
the sermon ought to be a most important part of
the service, but he also held that the Lord's

Supper [1] ought to be celebrated every Sunday [2] with solemn and orderly reverence, and that everyone who was there ought to partake of it. Those who were wilfully wicked or careless were forbidden to come to it, and were to be severely punished by the city officials at the bidding of the Church, unless they amended their lives.

It is difficult for us to realise what a hard task lay before Calvin. Farel had found Geneva full of horrible wickedness; drunkenness, gambling, and dishonesty were common enough, and there were other things, too bad to be written here. But Calvin's church was terribly strict, forbidding people some quite harmless pleasures, and interfering with their whole lives. It is not surprising that at the end of three years the citizens revolted, and Calvin had to leave Geneva. He settled for a while in Strasbourg, where he married and became pastor of the French Church. Two years later Geneva repented of its act and begged Calvin to come back again.

Through Calvin Geneva became a centre of Protestant learning. He established a theological college there under his friend Theodore Beza, wrote, lectured and preached in the city, sent out

[1] Protestants came to call the Eucharist the Lord's Supper, or the Sacrament. They disliked the word " Mass " because it reminded them of the things they held to be wrong in Catholic faith and worship.

[2] He could not get his followers to do this.

Bibles from the press, and wrote letters of counsel and encouragement to his friends in England and France and the Netherlands and Poland. His rule in the city was as stern as ever. His enemies fired guns under his windows at night and set dogs on him in the street, but nothing could make him less watchful and severe. When Servetus, a man who had written blasphemous books (and whom the Catholics in France had condemned to death), fled to Geneva, Calvin accused him to the City Council, and thought it right that he should be killed, though he tried hard to save him from the terrible death by burning, which was the usual punishment for heresy. Yet Calvin's friends knew his gentler and more human side. He played quoits and table games with them in his spare time; he could write consoling words to his friend, the Duchess of Ferrara, when her son-in-law died, though he had been Calvin's bitterest enemy; and he died asking pardon for his outbursts of anger.

Protestant refugees from all countries came to Geneva, among them John Knox, who was to do much to establish the Reformed Church in Scotland. They took away with them the faith of Calvin and his system of Church government. He taught them to respect the State, but as a servant of the Church, to which their first loyalty was due, and for whose honour and liberty they must be willing to die. He also taught them to fear God so greatly that they feared nothing and no one else, and were ready to overthrow all tyrannies in His Name. Calvinism sometimes made men hard and cruel, but it always made them strong, honest, straight-living lovers of civic freedom, and it was men like this who began to build up a new kind of Christian civilisation in Europe and America.

NOTES . . . .

THE PROTESTANTS IN FRANCE.—In 1534 a small group of fanatical Protestants had brought down a storm of persecution on themselves by putting up placards all over the city of Paris, insulting the Mass. The Catholics retaliated by treating their opponents with shocking cruelty, burning some of them alive. This persecution continued to rage. Protestants (who in France came to be called *Huguenots*) were killed in hundreds and their books burned; but they only increased the more, and became a strong political party led by Admiral COLIGNY and Prince LOUIS of CONDE. A massacre of Huguenots, after they had been promised protection, brought on a civil war in France. On St Bartholomew's Day, 1572, the Catholic King ordered a terrible massacre of Protestants in France, but the deed shocked all

Europe and only helped the cause he had tried to kill. These terrible wars of religion went on until at last a Huguenot prince inherited the throne. He formally accepted the Catholic faith in order to gain power and restore peace to his country, and then granted toleration to the Protestants by the Edict of Nantes in 1598.

THE PROTESTANTS IN THE NETHERLANDS suffered the most terrible persecution, especially during the reign of Philip II of Spain, who was their ruler, and the Duke of Alva, who carried out his decrees. They retaliated by destroying the images and pictures and all that could remind them of Catholic worship in the churches. Philip's answer was a worse persecution, but it did not succeed. Under the leadership of WILLIAM, the heroic PRINCE OF ORANGE, the Netherlands gained their freedom in face of overwhelming odds.

THE INQUISITION.—In the thirteenth century committees of inquiry, or *Inquisitions*, had been set up in France during the time of the Albigensian heresy to discover and punish heretics. At first they consisted of the parish priest and people of the district, but later the Pope appointed the Inquisitors. Heretics were condemned by the Church and then handed over to the civil authorities for punishment. Inquisitions were set up later in Italy, Spain, and the Netherlands, but never in England. The authorities inflicted torture and the most horrible cruelties on those suspected of heresy, particularly in Spain, where great spectacles were made of the burning of heretics in yellow robes on which were embroidered flames and devils. The Church did not invent, and never actually carried out these horrible acts: they were the ordinary punishments of cruel times (*cf*. Servetus). But the punishments became more cruel as the religious wars went on, and the fact that they were used and encouraged by the Church is a dark blot on the history of Christianity, and ought never to be excused. It is sad to think that the followers of St Dominic were generally among the inquisitors of these times.

The Inquisition made the very name of Catholic hated and dreaded by Protestants for centuries. Nevertheless, even in these dark times there were Catholics, as well as Protestants, who lived noble lives of heroism and self-sacrifice in the service of their Lord and of the Church. Such men were St IGNATIUS LOYOLA and St FRANCIS XAVIER.

CHAPTER XVIII
THE ROMAN CATHOLICS
Sixteenth Century
ST IGNATIUS LOYOLA, 1491–1556
ST FRANCIS XAVIER, 1506–1552

In the year 1521 a young Spanish knight, named Ignatius Loyola, was badly wounded in one of his country's battles with the French. During his illness he asked for books of romance to read, but those who nursed him brought him stories of the saints instead. It was these books which turned the Spanish soldier into a servant of Christ and the leader of an army of men who were to be teachers and missionaries in all parts of the world.

In preparation for his work Loyola spent a long time in a cave in thought and prayer; it was there that he made those prayers and meditations (*The Spiritual Exercises*), which were written down afterwards, and have been used by his followers ever since. To teach others he knew he must educate himself. He was not ashamed to learn Latin with the school children of Barcelona; then he went to two Spanish universities, and lastly to that at Paris. Here he gathered round him his first followers, who came to be known as the Company of Jesus, or the JESUITS.

The Jesuits set out to fight the evils of their time by preaching, by hearing confessions, helping the poor, and by teaching the Faith to children. They were especially bound to the service of the Pope, ready to go anywhere at his command and that of their leader (who was always called a General). Like other monks and friars, the Jesuits were unmarried, had no possessions except what the Order allowed them for their work, lived under discipline, and were vowed to even stricter obedience without murmur or complaint.

One of the first of Loyola's followers was Francis Xavier, a young noble from the hill country between France and Spain, and one of the greatest of all Christian missionaries. He had met Loyola at the Paris University, and served the Company gladly, tramping from France to Venice in the bitter cold, singing as he went, serving the poor in the Hospital for Incurables in that city, begging his way to Rome again, sleeping in rat-haunted cattle-sheds, and wading waist-deep through swollen rivers to reach it. When Loyola commanded him to go and preach the Gospel in India, where the Portuguese had possessions, he cried joyfully, " Here I am then—forward ! " The journey to India in a Portuguese ship was a terrible affair ; an almost shelterless deck, salt meat and musty biscuits to eat, bad water, and an outbreak of plague. It took thirteen months to get there, and the ship was becalmed in the tropics. But the well-born Spaniard spent his time in caring for the sick, cutting up their food, washing their clothes, and giving them what comfort he could.

They landed at Goa, where one of his most difficult tasks was the winning of bad, dishonest Portuguese officials back to a Christian life. From there he went inland, preaching, teaching, and baptising children. He was the kind of man whom all children loved, and he taught them to help him, singing Christian hymns, carrying his messages, and going with him sometimes when he preached. Xavier translated [1] the Lord's Prayer, the Apostles' Creed, the Ten Commandments, the Hail Mary, and other prayers into the language of the South Indian people. His disciples became missionaries in Ceylon, whilst he travelled to Malacca and eastwards to Japan. Here again he did not know the language, and had to preach through interpreters; yet three powerful Japanese nobles were converted by his life and teaching. In 1552 he sailed from India to China, and in December reached the island of San Chan, off the coast. But the hardships of his life, and the terrible strain of his journeys, now told on him, and in that lonely spot the noble

---

[1] With difficulty, and by means of interpreters. He never learnt the language.

missionary passed away, his heart going out to the vast land he had longed to enter, and on his lips the words, " Farther yet."

NOTES . . . .

THE JESUITS.—The heroism and the tireless work of the Jesuits drew many men into their ranks—before Loyola died there were a thousand of them—and during the next two hundred years their numbers steadily increased. They went out as missionaries to India and China and Japan, to Brazil and Florida and Mexico and Peru, winning men to the Faith by their life and teaching, and gladly suffering martyrdom for their cause. Later they established missions in Canada and around the Great Lakes, where two of their heroic leaders, BREBEUF and DANIEL, were tortured and killed by the Huron Indians, and where MARQUETTE and JOLIET brought the Faith to the Indians of Illinois.

The Jesuits built great churches, very rich and ornate. They also established famous schools, which for some time provided the best education that was to be had anywhere.

But there is another side to the story of the Jesuits. In their determination to do their work they sometimes used methods which were not Christian at all, and in the days of their wealth and power they interfered in political and commercial affairs to such an extent that they came to be feared and hated not only by Protestants, but by Catholics too. They got a name for being crafty and deceitful and ready to use any method, however bad, to gain their ends. In India and China Jesuit missionaries, who had almost become heathens themselves in order to gain the people, had to be suppressed. They were expelled from Catholic France and Portugal, and in 1773 the Pope himself abolished them, " recognizing that . . . for the welfare of Christendom it were better that the Order should disappear." Forty years later they were re-established.

OTHER CATHOLIC REFORMERS.—Other Spaniards besides Loyola tried to serve and reform the Catholic Church. Among them were CARDINAL XIMENES, who published the whole Bible in five languages, and helped the Dominican missionary, BARTHOLOMEW LAS CASAS, in his fight against the cruelties of the Spanish slave-owners in the newly discovered lands of America ; ST TERESA (1515-1582) and ST JOHN OF THE CROSS (1542-1591), who persuaded many Spanish monks and nuns to a stricter and purer way of living, and wrote books on prayer and spiritual experience.

THE COUNCIL OF TRENT.—In the previous century two Church Councils had tried to set right some of the terrible evils of the times, and during the lifetime of Luther and Calvin Protestants and Catholics had met more than once in conference and vainly tried to reach an agreement. All these efforts failed because of the wars between European rulers, the religious persecutions, and the quarrels between the Pope and the bishops. At the Council of Trent, which lasted from 1545 to 1563, only Catholics were present, and its discussions were largely in the hands of the Italian bishops and the Jesuits, whose great aim was to exalt the power and authority of the Pope. All new Protestant teachings were condemned, and it was stated that the traditional beliefs handed down by the Church were as important as the teaching of the Bible. Catholics were only permitted to read this in the old (Vulgate) version, and it was decided that an " index " should be made naming those writings which contained wrong ideas and forbidding them to be printed or read. The Council stated the Catholic beliefs of the time clearly and carefully, explaining some which had been misunderstood ; it insisted that bishops should preach or provide preachers for their people, and that they should not live luxuriously and spend the Church's money on their relatives. Most important of all, it established a system like that of the old Episcopal schools, and from this time onwards Catholic priests were taught and trained in seminaries under the charge of their bishops.

THE ROMAN CATHOLIC CHURCH.—By these methods, and with the help of the Jesuits, the Catholics began to regain many people who had become, or would have become, Protestants. But from this time the character of the Catholic Church was changed; it became narrower in outlook, always suspicious of heresy, and attributed more and more authority and power to the Pope. Those outside it, who rejected the supremacy of the Pope, came to feel that this part of the Church had no right to call itself simply *Catholic*, since it did not represent the whole body of Christian people, and, from their standpoint, it had corrupted the early faith of the Christians. In England, before 1600, the supporters of the Pope began to be called ROMAN CATHOLICS, and this is their official title in England to-day.

6

CHAPTER XIX

THE CHURCH OF ENGLAND
SIXTEENTH CENTURY
THOMAS CRANMER, 1489–1556

FOR over a century after Henry VIII repudiated the Pope, three parties struggled to reform the English Church in their own way. The Catholics, while wanting to reform the old abuses, wished to restore the Papal supremacy; the Protestants wanted to destroy everything that reminded them of Catholicism. But there was a third party who felt that the Pope had no right to the power and authority he claimed in England, yet that the English Church was truly Catholic, and whilst getting rid of many abuses, ought to keep the main beliefs and ceremonies of the old religion. Unfortunately these men linked their cause to the idea of the Royal supremacy, and thus brought the Church into a bondage to the State from which it is not wholly free to-day.[1]

[1] This is true only in England. When Englishmen established colonies abroad they took their Church with them, but it became a self-governing Church, free from State control. This kind of English Episcopal Church is found now in America, Canada, Australia, New Zealand, India, South Africa, the West Indies,

Each of these three parties gained power in turn.

In the reign of the boy-king, Edward VI, the Protestants had the upper hand. John Knox, the Calvinist, became the King's chaplain, and many foreign Protestants were given positions of importance in England. In London and some other places the altars of the churches were destroyed. The men who ruled for the young King seized not only the treasures of the churches, but the money that belonged to almshouses and hospitals, clubs and guilds. Libraries were plundered and burned, lectureships suppressed, and parishes disendowed. A few grammar schools were erected as an excuse for this, but most of the money went to enrich the robber-rulers of England. Some of this pillage was due to Protestant principles, but most of it to men who found in Protestantism a convenient excuse for getting what they wanted.

In Mary's reign the pendulum swung to the other extreme, and the Catholics were in power. The Queen became a gloomy religious fanatic, and persecuted Protestants. By burning them as heretics she made all England hate and fear the religion she professed.

In Elizabeth's reign the middle party came into

China, and Japan. In Ireland and Wales the English Church has been disestablished ; in Scotland it has never been the Established Church.

power, and the Church of England took on a definite character of its own.[1]   It was Protestant in repudiating the claims of the Pope and some of the later Catholic beliefs.   But it was Catholic in keeping the main beliefs and ceremonies of the old Church ; its new Archbishop, Mathew Parker, was consecrated by men who were themselves in the Apostolic Succession ; the Nicene Creed was sung at its altars, and it established a Prayer Book in which, though considerably revised, there appeared the old Hours and the old Liturgy of the Catholic Church.

In these disturbed and confused times it is not surprising that there is no one great heroic person who stands for the English Church in the same way that Calvin stands for the Church at Geneva. Perhaps the most important churchman of the times was Thomas Cranmer, and his story is mostly a very sad one.   He was the slave and tool of Henry VIII, his views were influenced by every party in power, and he recanted his faith in abject terms when he was confronted by persecution. Yet he did two great things for which the English Church is in his debt, and all men honour him.   He wrote the Litany, and the first of the English Prayer Books on which all the others are based ; and he died, at last, an honest and heroic man.

[1] This is called the Elizabethan Settlement.

Cranmer's Prayer Book, written in magnificent English, was composed of the old services known and loved by the people, shortened and simplified, with additions from still older sources.

By this time some reform of the Church services was badly needed. There had come to be a number of books in use, one for each part of a service, and one for each person who took any special part. One was for the priest, another for the deacon, several for the singers. There was also a Calendar, books of selected readings, and many more. Some of the services were used differently in different parts of England, the Hours had become terribly long and complicated, only parts of the Bible were read in a rather scrappy way, and some not very satisfactory stories of the saints were included.

In Cranmer's Prayer Book the Hours were reduced to two, Mattins and Evensong and the Bible readings were arranged in an orderly way so that the whole Bible was read through once a year, and only Bible readings were used. The Prayer Book contained the Services of Baptism, Confirmation (with Catechism), Marriage, the Visitation and Anointing of the Sick, the Burial Service, and others. Its Communion Service was based on that English Mass which was best known and loved, *The Sarum Liturgy*, with some additions from older sources, and it directed the priest to wear the ceremonial dress [1] of the Church. One of the most interesting things in the book was a note saying that worshippers might say their prayers in the way that helped them most: they might kneel and make the sign of the Cross, or remain still, just as they pleased. But this Prayer Book, published in 1549, was too fair-minded for the violent persecuting Churchmen of Edward VI's reign. The Protestants, who were then in power, insisted on Cranmer revising it—though he would not do all that they wished—and they made a bad business of it. Many of the Reformers neither understood the making of public services nor the meaning of the old rites: they were simply obsessed with the idea that everything in the old Catholic service book was wrong. This Second Prayer Book was not consented to by the English Church as a whole, and was only used in some parts of the country for eight months. Then the boy-king died. Queen Mary brought to England a fierce, persecuting Roman Catholicism. One after another men and women suffered the terrible death by burning which the heresy laws demanded, and England grew to hate Mary's religion as it had never hated any other. In the year 1555 two famous Protestants were burned, Bishop Ridley and Hugh Latimer, the great English preacher. Cranmer was made to see

[1] Generally spoken of as vestments   See p. 210.

them die; everything was done to make him recant, and it was hinted that he might save his life if he did. He had been imprisoned himself for two years, he was old and ill, and he gave in. He signed a document repudiating his past beliefs and submitting to the Pope.

But his persecutors never meant him to live, and he was commanded to read this document in public before he was burned.

In St Mary's Church, Oxford, Cranmer stood up in an old ragged gown, his paper in his hand, and began to read it. But when he came to the word " renounce," he suddenly looked up, and all the cowardice and weakness of his past life passed from him. Slowly and deliberately he said, " I renounce and refuse all things written with my hand contrary to the truth I thought in my heart and writ for fear of death . . . and as for the Pope, I refuse him as Christ's enemy and anti-Christ, with all his false doctrines." Amid cries of anger and wonder and sympathy he was dragged from the platform on which he stood. He shook himself free from his gaolers and ran to the stake outside. He thrust the hand that had signed the document into the flames. " This hand hath offended," he cried, and then was silent. The end came mercifully soon.

NOTES . . .

THE ELIZABETHAN SETTLEMENT.—In Elizabeth's reign the Church was faced with tremendous difficulties. On the one hand, the Pope excommunicated the Queen (1570), and called on her subjects to rebel against her, thus forcing her to treat all Roman Catholics as traitors. On the other hand, the extreme Protestants refused to obey the moderate laws issued concerning Church worship, they pulled down altars, abolished vestments and ornaments, and nearly succeeded in making the services like those of Calvin at Geneva. Yet before the end of her reign the settlement was reached, and a Third Prayer Book was issued, which, though it was not so good as the first, was such that the majority of English Churchmen could use it. Scholars like Bishops JEWEL and HOOKER and ANDREWES wrote books to explain and defend the English Church. The *Private Prayers* of Bishop Andrewes have become famous.

THE ENGLISH BIBLE.—Since Cædmon made Bible stories into Anglo-Saxon songs, and Bede translated the Gospel of St John at Jarrow, there had been many attempts to give the English people the Bible in their own language. Of these JOHN WYCLIF was the first to distribute manuscript copies in any number, through his Poor Preachers. About a century later WILLIAM TYNDALE (1484-

1536) translated it directly from the Greek, using the Greek New Testament of Erasmus. Tyndale had to translate and print part of his Bible in Antwerp where he fled to escape persecution. Catholics saw that men were coming to doubt some of their beliefs and to think that the claims of the clergy were wrong through reading the Bible for themselves in their own language ; they therefore tried to stop private translations, and wished to provide their own version and their own explanation of it. Protestants believed that the book could be trusted to tell the truth and should be put into everyone's hands, though they, too, often wrote notes in its margins to explain their especial beliefs. Tyndale worked at his translation in great difficulties and danger ; he was finally discovered, caught, and put to death by his opponents. But his splendid translation did not perish, under cover of someone else's name it was used by Miles Coverdale for the GREAT BIBLE he prepared for Cranmer. This is the Bible which was set up in the English churches. It was revised again in Elizabeth's reign, not very well, by the Bishops (BISHOPS' BIBLE). But the majority of the people used and loved the GENEVA BIBLE, which was practically Tyndale's Bible, divided into verses, well bound and printed in small clear type by the English Protestants in Geneva. This Bible had notes in its margins urging readers to accept the views of the Reformers. The Roman Catholics had an English translation, too, also with notes, based on the Vulgate (the DOUAI BIBLE). In James the First's reign (when a Fourth Prayer Book was also issued), it was suggested that a new Bible translation should be made. The King was enthusiastic. Forty-seven scholars of very varied opinions in Church matters worked in three companies at Oxford, Cambridge, and Westminster, and produced in 1611 one of the world's greatest books, the Authorised Version of the Bible in the English language.

The book was written in the finest English that has ever been spoken, it had no notes in it urging men to belong to this or that party in the Church, and it came to be the one book which nearly every household in England possessed.

CHAPTER XX

THE FREE CHURCHES
SEVENTEENTH CENTURY
JOHN ROBINSON, 1575–1625

THE man who first suggested to James I that a new translation of the Bible should be made was a leader of the extreme Protestant or *Puritan* party in the Church of England. The Puritans were so-called because of the strictness of their lives. Some of them preferred *Episcopacy* (government by Bishops) though they did not hold it essential to the Church ; others wanted to establish Presbyterianism, and some thought that the Church should consist of groups of Christian people who elected their own pastors, and were free to worship as they thought right without the interference of the State or of any central Church authority. These last, because they separated from the rest into independent congregations, were called, first, Separatists, then Independents, then CONGREGATIONALISTS.

The Puritans disliked all outward ceremony in worship, all set forms of prayer, all symbols and decorations in churches, and even such acts and gestures as kneeling and making the sign of the Cross. They, like Calvin, thought that the Church should only consist of people who were outwardly living a Christian life, and that the lives of individuals should be watched over by their pastor and other officials of the Church. So it came about that the Puritans were temperate, honest, pure, and strong, there were no drunkards or cheats or evil-living men among them ; yet they were sometimes narrow-minded, Pharisaical and interfering. Their careful preaching taught their people well, but their churches often looked more like gloomy lecture halls than places of worship. Just as the Church of the Middle Ages had swung to one extreme, so they swung to the other.

The Puritans, like the other parties in the Church of England, suffered persecution, especially those Separatists, who, in Queen Elizabeth's reign, boldly condemned State interference in the Church. Separatist congregations gathered round Robert Browne in the eastern counties, where the memory of the teaching of Wyclif's Lollards was still strong. Browne was suppressed and imprisoned, and other fearless witnesses to the idea of a Free Church suffered death for their convictions : Henry Barrowe, John Greenwood, and John Penry. Some of Barrowe's followers fled to Amsterdam, in Holland, the most tolerant of Protestant countries.

In the seventeenth century two small congregations of Separatists used to meet at Gainsborough and Scrooby, in Lincolnshire; among them were William Brewster, William Bradford, John Smyth, Thomas Helwys, and John Robinson, who became one of the most famous of them. He had been educated at Oxford, and had been a curate at Norwich before he became a Separatist.

Persecution, fines, and imprisonment drove these men to follow those who had fled to Holland. Their flight was a desperate one, for the ports were watched. The captain of the first ship they hired betrayed them into the hands of the officers of the law, who seized their books and money and possessions. The second time they tried to escape they were surprised by soldiers when only a boat-load had got aboard. Yet at last, some by one ship and some by another, they got across and joined the rest of the Separatists at Amsterdam. John Robinson was one of the last to go, for he stayed to help the weakest to get across.

They found the Church members at Amsterdam rather a difficult and quarrelsome set of people, who were terribly upset because their pastor's wife used scent and wore a " toping " hat, and had furious arguments as to whether Aaron's breastplate was sea-green or blue !

After the second lot of Separatists had arrived, some of them wanted to establish a Presbyterian form of Church government, and John Smyth began to declare that the baptism of infants could not mean anything, and that those so baptised ought to have it done again. John Robinson hated quarrels, and he did not want to disagree with other Churches more than he could help, nor did he want to abuse the kind hospitality of the Dutch by making a turmoil in Amsterdam. So in the year 1609 he and some others moved to Leyden, where they bought a large house.[1] The big room served them for church and meeting-room, and he (as their pastor), with his wife and family, lived upstairs. This church met on Sunday mornings to celebrate the Lord's Supper, and for worship and preaching, and in the afternoons there was another meeting when members of the congregation might also speak if they felt that God had given them anything to say. At other times the church met to discuss the conduct of its members and their week-day affairs. Here their pastor was a great help to them, for he was an educated man and knew how to deal with the Dutch officials and the city laws.

The Separatist church at Leyden was very happy. "They lived together in love and peace all their days," said William Bradford, who was one of them. John Robinson gave something of his own

[1] In 1616 Henry Jacob set up the first Congregational Church in London.

wise, tolerant spirit to his people. He knew that those who have been persecuted sometimes become as narrow and cruel as their persecutors, so he encouraged them to be friendly with other churches. Members of his congregation, who could understand Dutch sometimes worshipped in the Dutch Reformed Church, Presbyterians were welcomed at Leyden, and no member of the Church of England who joined John Robinson's church was made to feel that his old Church had been wicked and shameful.

But life in Holland was hard on the English refugees. They had to take any work they could get to make a living, and even here the persecution in England touched them sometimes, and the printing of their books was stopped. Rumours of a war with Spain, which would immediately affect the city of Leyden, made them face the possibility of another flight. They began to dream of founding a colony in the new world of America, where they might worship in peace and freedom, bring fresh glory to their home-land, and preach the Gospel to the native tribes. They decided that a company of the strongest and most suitable should go first, and that later their pastor should join them.

Before they went John Robinson gave them some words of advice, for he knew that at first the life of the settlers in America would be even harder than it had been in Holland. He told them to be loyal and kindly to one another, to respect and obey the leaders they elected, and above all, to follow whatever truth God should reveal to them. John Robinson saw the world in a state of terrible confusion, and he did not believe that even Luther and Calvin knew all the truth. So he said, " Follow me no further than you have seen me follow the Lord Jesus Christ. Be ready to receive whatever truth shall be made known to you from the written word of God. I am very persuaded that the Lord has more truth yet to break forth out of His Holy Word."

In the summer of 1620 the *Speedwell* set sail from Holland to England, there to join the *Mayflower* and embark for America.

Thus the " Pilgrim Fathers " began their great adventure, but before five years were over John Robinson had peacefully passed away. He gave something of his very self to the New World of the West, a spirit of steady endurance, a love of peaceful freedom, and a faith that, in the unknown and the untried, God waits to give good things and to reveal more of His truth and His will.

NOTES . . . .

THE PILGRIM FATHERS IN AMERICA.—Though two ships set out from Plymouth, one was found unseaworthy, and had to return. Some of her passengers crowded into the *Mayflower*; others, together with the much-needed ship, some tools and implements, had to be left behind. For nine weeks the ship tossed on stormy seas, then the settlers landed, calling their colony and the bay in which they settled by the name of the port from which they had sailed, *Plymouth*.

Two friendly Indians, SAMOSET and SQUANTO, taught them to plant and manure corn Indian-wise, to fish and hunt and explore, and they made a treaty of peace with the nearest friendly tribe. JOHN CARVER, and after him WILLIAM BRADFORD, became their governors, MILES STANDISH their military leader in case of attack from unfriendly Indians.

Exposure and hard work brought disease and death, and in the first four months forty-four out of the one hundred and two settlers had died. Supplies of corn grew short, there was trouble with unfriendly Indians, and other colonists who joined them were often of a poor sort and badly equipped for a settler's life. It was difficult to send back enough goods to pay the shipping company who had brought them out. Yet the little colony survived and prospered, bound to-

gether by faith and friendship, and the compact
they had made on board ship to " frame such just
and equal laws . . . as shall be thought most
meet and convenient for the general good."
In Plymouth Colony, though everyone was a
Church member, yet Church and State were
separate.

The Puritan colonies which were founded
later had a State-Established Church, and were
much stricter in their ways than Plymouth.
JOHN ENDICOTT (1628) founded *Salem*; JOHN
WINTHROP (1630) came out to *Massachusetts*
with a large and well-equipped party of settlers,
and from this settlement sprang the neighbouring
Puritan colonies of *Newhaven* and *Connecticutt*.
Providence was founded by ROGER WILLIAMS,
and there all who would not conform to the ways
of Plymouth or the Puritan colonies found a
home.

THE BAPTISTS.—John Smyth and Thomas
Helwys were the founders and the first leaders
of the BAPTISTS, so-called because of their views
about Baptism. They held that only people who
had declared their belief in Jesus Christ should be
baptised, and that it should be done as the first
Christians did it, by immersion (see p. 6). Their
Church government and worship was like that of
the Independents. 'It was two Baptists, LEONARD
BUSHER and JOHN MURTON, who were the first

men to write pamphlets pleading for full liberty of conscience in England.

The most famous Baptist of these times was JOHN BUNYAN, the Bedford tinker, who was imprisoned for his fearless preaching in Charles the Second's reign. He wrote *The Pilgrim's Progress*, an allegory, or picture-tale, of the spiritual life of Christian people, their battles and dangers and temptations and comforts on the straight road that leads to Eternal Life. This book has been translated into a great many languages, and is read and loved by Christians of all denominations.

THE INDEPENDENTS IN ENGLAND.—While the American colonies were developing, the Puritans were gaining power in England. The anti-Puritan party had become closely associated with the fortunes and politics of the Stuart kings, and when Charles I was beheaded, its bishops were imprisoned, and Episcopacy and the Prayer Book were abolished. Cromwell's men broke up the statues and stained glass and organs in the churches, and destroyed the vestments of the clergy, sometimes leaving nothing but the shell of the glorious churches of the Middle Ages. Though the Protector treated his enemies in Church and State thus, he was more tolerant than most men of his time. All sorts of Protestants—Puritans, Presbyterians, Independents—held office in the Church during his Protectorate, although they all had to be approved by a committee of " Triers." Some of the most famous of these clergy were RICHARD BAXTER, JOHN OWEN, THOMAS GOODWIN, and JOHN HOWE.

With the Restoration of Charles II there was a complete change. The Bishops and the Prayer Book were restored, and an Act of Uniformity passed. This Act demanded that all clergy should accept everything contained in the Prayer Book, should not minister in the Church of England unless ordained by a bishop, nor teach as a tutor or schoolmaster without his permission, should renounce the Solemn League and Covenant,[1] and swear never to take up arms against the King or his ministers. No mercy was shown to those who refused to accept these terms. They were driven out of their livings without even the small amount which had been allowed to those whom the Puritans had turned out: they were forbidden to teach, and no one was allowed to collect money to help them.

The great majority of the clergy, about two thousand of them, refused to take the oath, and with heroic and splendid courage faced imprisonment and starvation rather than act against their conscience. They preached in the fields, suffered in prison, or worked, half-starved, at any job to

[1] See p. 181.

support their wives and children. Because of their refusal to conform to the Act they became known as NONCONFORMISTS or DISSENTERS.

During Cromwell's Protectorate there arose a new group of people who had different views from all the organised Churches of their day. It was founded by GEORGE FOX, and called THE SOCIETY OF FRIENDS.

CHAPTER XXI

THE SOCIETY OF FRIENDS
SEVENTEENTH CENTURY
GEORGE FOX, 1624–1691

IN 1648, and the years that followed, a big man, with long curly hair and strangely piercing eyes, dressed in homespun coat and leather breeches, tramped to and fro in the Midland and Northern English counties preaching to the people. It was new and strange preaching. He told them that everyone had within himself a Light by which he could know the truth and do Christ's will, and that all the ordinary ways and practices of church-going folk were unnecessary—their church build-ings and holydays, their paid and educated ministers, their set prayers and their sacraments. He told people to swear no oaths, since Christ had forbidden it, to raise their hats to no man since this encouraged foolish pride, and to take no part in war, since that was against the peaceful and forgiving spirit of Christian people.

George Fox did not only preach in the fields and in houses. In 1649 he began to enter the " steeple-houses," as he called the churches, and cry out with his great voice against all that was said and done there. It is not very surprising that the magistrates put him in prison, and that angry mobs sometimes stoned and beat him and chased him away. They thought his refusal to take off his hat an insult, his refusal to swear oaths disloyal, and they could not understand his words about the wickedness of war when England was being practically ruled by Cromwell's victorious army. Moreover, the civil authorities were suspicious of people like this; there had been many strange prophets on the Continent, some [1] of whom had fallen into all sorts of wickedness through following their own opinions. So Fox was tried by many an angry magistrate, and saw the inside of many of the dark, evil-smelling prisons of his times.

But there was something about the steady, peaceful courage of this man which made many people listen to him and like him, and great numbers of people became his disciples. He married Margaret Fell of Swarthmore Hall, who shared his faith, and sometimes his imprisonments. He travelled all over England, and to Scotland and Wales.

When the Stuarts were restored, two cruel Acts

[1] Especially some called the ANA-BAPTISTS who had shocked all Europe by their lawlessness. These are not the same as the Baptists mentioned in the last chapter.

were passed against all Dissenters—the Conventicle Act, 1664, which forbade the meeting of more than five people for worship other than that ordained by the Church of England ; and the Five Mile Act, 1665, which forbade Dissenters to stay within five miles of any town, thus preventing them from earning a living by teaching. Hundreds of Dissenters of all kinds were imprisoned during those times in the dreadful gaols of England, and many died of hunger and disease.

The followers of Fox, who came to be called " The Society of Friends," were persecuted with the rest, but their behaviour puzzled the officers who arrested them more than that of any of the others. They would sit quietly, listening for the Holy Spirit to speak to them, in a plainly furnished room [1] with no ornaments or symbols, and when they were roughly handled and turned out of doors, their room wrecked, they would offer no resistance, but come back quietly and sit down among the ruins. It was difficult to know how to deal with such people.

Not all Friends were like this. Some [2] raved wildly ; others thought that because they had the Inner Light everything that they did was right, and one man even declared that he was

---

[1] Friends call their places of worship " Meeting-houses."

[2] They were sometimes called Ranters or Quakers because of their excitable ways.

Christ. Such people were likely to be found among those who had abolished the discipline and laws of the older Churches, and especially among the Friends, who as yet acknowledged no Church rules at all.

George Fox saw these dangers, and he decided that there must be some kind of assembly in which Friends could declare plainly what their Society stood for. So he organised monthly and quarterly meetings for the small groups in parishes and counties, and a great yearly meeting which was to be a sort of parliament, and the Society has been organised in this way ever since.

For the same reason he went to America in 1671. Some Friends there had been persecuted and even put to death in the Puritan colonies, and they were not much liked or understood in the others, so he determined to show them and their neighbours what being a Friend really meant. His ship was chased by pirates, and he made many a rough journey in an open boat, and through thick woods where the wolves howled round his camp-fire at night, preaching his faith, and even getting Red Indians to come to his meetings.

When he got back to England he met with persecution again, but not for long. He lived to see a tolerant, kindly Dutchman on the throne of England, and died peacefully among his friends.

Two of the most famous of Fox's followers were Robert Barclay (1648-1690), who wrote an *Apology*, explaining the beliefs of the Society; and William Penn (1644-1718), who founded the American colony of Pennsylvania. Penn's justice in dealing with the Red Indians, and his friendship with them, will always be remembered with pride, both by Friends and by Englishmen.

Members of the Society continued to follow its founder's teaching; they wore plain, sober-coloured clothes, and treated everyone [1] with the same respect whatever their social position. Women as well as men took part in the meetings. Their reverence for every human being because of the Inner Light which dwells in him, made them among the first people to condemn slavery and bad prison conditions. They have always been ready to give help in any sort of distress in every land and to every race and class of people.

NOTES   .   .   .   .

THE CHURCH OF ENGLAND.—While the Puritans were trying to make the English Church like the Reformed Continental Churches, other English Churchmen were trying equally hard to keep it

---

[1] They called everyone " thou," when " you " was used in addressing important people. Kings—and editors—still say " we."

Catholic. In the reign of Charles I, Archbishop Laud determined to restore something of the old Catholic worship, and hoped and believed and worked for a united Catholic Church in Europe. His sympathy with the Roman Catholics (though he repudiated the Papal Supremacy) infuriated the Puritans.

Laud tried to enforce his views by harsh methods of persecution in both England and Scotland; they failed, and he was beheaded. Yet he died for his Church, and the things he did were not forgotten. The Long Parliament which beheaded him legalised a Book of Discipline and the West-minster Catechism, which aimed at making England Calvinist, but its plans did not succeed. In the reign of Charles II the two parties in the Church met at the Savoy Conference, and there, though some of the things the Puritans asked for were agreed upon, the English Church resolutely re-fused to make its teaching and worship like those of the Presbyterians. In the same year the Prayer Book was revised (the Fifth Prayer Book), and this is the book the English Church uses to-day.

But whilst the English Church refused to be like the Reformed Churches, it also refused to be made Roman Catholic. James the Second's attempts to fill all the important offices in Church and State with Roman Catholics were resented, and when he tried to issue laws on their behalf against the will of his Parliament, all England rose against him. The Archbishop of Canterbury (SANCROFT) and six bishops withstood the King, and were imprisoned for it. They were released and hailed with joy by the people, and for a while Churchmen and Dissenters stood together in sympathy. The King failed, and fled from the country. How the Stuarts failed to enforce their will on the people of Scotland is told in the story of the COVENANTERS.

CHAPTER XXII

THE CHURCH OF SCOTLAND
SEVENTEENTH CENTURY
THE COVENANTERS

SCOTLAND had been evangelised mainly by St Ninian, St Columba, and St Kentigern, and it kept the Irish customs till the eighth century, when it began to accept those of Rome, as England had already done. This was largely through St Margaret of Scotland, a Saxon who married the Scottish king, Malcolm, and brought with her many of the kindlier and more civilised customs of the South. Under her descendants the land was divided into dioceses, and Benedictine monasteries were established.

As the Archbishops of Canterbury and York were continually quarrelling as to who should appoint the Scottish Bishops, Scotland decided to settle the matter for itself by appealing directly to the Pope. But in time the people came to resent his heavy taxation, and a revolt against the Papacy took place. Wyclif's Lollards found their way into Scotland and were suppressed; Patrick Hamilton, the young Abbot of Ferns, was burnt as a Lutheran heretic in 1528, and George Wishart in 1543, but Cardinal Beaton, who arrested him, was assassinated, and a civil war broke out. It was in this war that John Knox was taken prisoner and sent to France to serve as a galley-slave; he was released, and after visiting Frankfort and Geneva, he came back to his own country to preach the Reformed Faith again, savagely and relentlessly attacking the Catholic Church.

Scotland established Protestantism by Act of Parliament in 1560, and by 1592 Presbyterianism was made the religion of the country, largely through Andrew Melville. The Church was governed by presbyteries and local synods, and the great Church Assembly, which met yearly. Those who would not conform to the laws of the Church were punished by fines and imprisonment, banishment, torture, or death, but the Presbyterians were more lenient in carrying out these punishments than their opponents had been.

The Stuart kings were determined to establish in Scotland an Episcopal Church of the same character as that of England, and as much under the royal control. Scottish bishops came to England to be consecrated, and were then given positions of importance in their own country. In Charles the First's reign a Prayer Book (very like the First English Prayer Book) was ordered to be used, and this was done by Royal Decree, and without any consultation of the Scottish Parliament or the Church Assembly. Scotland rose to defend, not only Presbyterianism, which was the religion of the majority of the people, but the rights and liberties of the nation itself. Vast crowds of people gathered to the church of the Grey Friars at Edinburgh and signed the *National Covenant*,[1] declaring that they would stand by their Church and their freedom, and Presbyterianism was again proclaimed the religion of Scotland (1638). It nearly became the religion of England, too, for the Presbyterians and Puritans joined forces to overthrow the King's power, and entered into an agreement to establish the Reformed Faith in Great Britain. Learned Scottish ministers, Henderson, Baillie, Gillespie, and Samuel Rutherford [2] came to the Westminster Assembly to prepare the Catechism and Book of Discipline (p. 177), but the restoration of Charles II put an end to all these plans.

The attempt to force Episcopacy and a Prayer Book on Scotland began all over again, and in this reign and the next the Covenanters were cruelly persecuted. Soldiers were quartered on the districts where they were known to gather for

[1] There had been " Covenants " or agreements before this, and the one entered into by Puritans and Presbyterians later was called " The Solemn League and Covenant."

[2] The *Letters* he wrote to his friends about the love of Christ are still read to-day.

worship, their ministers were hunted into the
moors and the desolate hills to starve, or shot
without mercy, since preaching at or attending a
Presbyterian service had become punishable by
death.

The Covenanters were liberty-loving patriots,
fierce, narrow-minded, and as ready to persecute
members of other Churches as they were to defend
and suffer for their own. But their defence of
the Church (as they believed Christ had meant it
to be constituted) is a great story, and there were
splendid and saintly men and women among them.

"My Lords," said the Presbyterian minister,
James Guthrie, who was sentenced to be hanged
at Edinburgh in 1661, "my conscience I cannot
submit, but this old crazy body and mortal flesh I
do submit to do with it whatsoever you will.   Only
I beseech you to ponder well what profit there is
in my blood; it is not the extinguishing of me, or
many others, that will extinguish the Covenant."
He spoke the truth.   Twenty years later Daniel
Cargill went to his execution, and, with his foot
on the gallows-ladder, cried proudly, "Lord knows
I go up this ladder with less fear and perturbation
than ever I entered a pulpit to preach."   A few
years later still, two women, Margaret Lauchlan
and Margaret Wilson, were condemned to be tied
to a stake in the Solway Firth and drowned by the
rising tide, and a third, Margaret Maxwell, to be

scourged through the streets of Wigtown for three days by the public executioner as an example to the people. But the people honoured her by shutting their doors and windows so as not to see her suffering, and even the children kept away, from the streets.

The persecuted Covenanters fled into the hills and the boggy moors, where the King's soldiers tried to seek them out. They gathered round their preachers in the open air, and sometimes took their Sacrament solemnly together in these wild places, knowing they might never share another on this earth. Alexander Peden was one of their preachers, " the Prophet," he was sometimes called, for he had the second sight, and could often tell of things before they came to pass. It is told how he fled the soldiers on his horse, swimming through rough waters, hiding in barns and caves, and once lying, too ill to move, hidden by the high-standing corn. He risked his life continually to preach to his people or to save them. There was John Semple and John Welwood, James Renwick and Richard Cameron, who fell fighting the King's men at Aird's Moss, and whose followers long afterwards were called by his name. One of the last of the famous Covenanters was Patrick Walker, who was not a preacher, but collected the stories of these men and wrote them down for us.

Walker lived to see the battle ended, and the Presbyterians again in power. Though in later times both Episcopalians and Roman Catholics were allowed to worship in peace and freedom, the Church the Covenanters fought and suffered for became, and still is, the Established Church of Scotland.

NOTES · · · ·

THE PSALMS were for many years the only hymns sung in the Presbyterian churches. They had been used daily by the Catholic Church, and many people knew them who knew no other Old Testament Scripture. In the sixteenth century a French poet, CLEMENT MAROT, began to translate them into French verse, and they were set to popular tunes. Calvin published some of these, as well as some of his own, in a book for Church worship, and Beza made others. These Psalms were sung by the Huguenot martyrs as they went to their death, and, through John Knox, they became the Hymn Book of the Scottish Church. English metrical psalms began to be sung in Edward VI's reign, and there was a complete version of them in 1562 (Daye's Psalter). Another writer of metrical psalms was WILLIAM KETHE (*All people that on earth do dwell*).

When Cranmer made his Prayer Book, he did

not think he could translate the old hymns well enough, so there was only one hymn (*Come, Holy Ghost*) in the Prayer Book, and the English Church for a while sang little else but Psalms.

THE NON-JURORS.—When William III came to the throne many of the best Scottish and English bishops refused to take the oath of allegiance to him, believing that kings were appointed by God as surely as bishops, and that only direct descendants of the king had a right to rule. These "Non-Jurors" were deprived of their Sees, and, in the English Church, the slack and easy-going bishops who were left in power got the name of Latitudinarians.

ARMINIUS, 1560-1609.—At the end of the sixteenth century a great controversy arose between those who believed in Calvin's theory of Predestination (p. 139) and the followers of a Dutchman named Arminius, who held opposite views. Arminius believed that man's salvation depended on his turning to God and accepting the help of His Holy Spirit. The Presbyterians, and most of the Independents, followed Calvin, but the English Church on the whole came to be Arminian.

THE ROMAN CATHOLICS.—While Puritans and Presbyterians and Episcopalians had been persecuting each other in turn in England and Scotland, the Roman Catholics had been persecuted nearly all the time. Queen Elizabeth fined and imprisoned and drove them out of the country, but many great houses had secret " priests' chambers," and heroic Jesuits from the Continent continually braved the authorities and risked torture and death to bring the Faith and the Sacrament to Britain. In the wild Highlands of Scotland they escaped capture more easily, and there were many Roman Catholics in that country even in the days when to say Mass in a private house was punishable by death. In Roman Catholic countries an effort was made to carry on the work begun at the Council of Trent; the monastic orders were reformed, clergy were trained, and the people more clearly and carefully taught the Faith they professed. The Church also helped and relieved the poor. In the seventeenth century there lived in France a Roman Catholic priest whose work for the poor will never be forgotten. His name was VINCENT DE PAUL.

CHAPTER XXIII

CHRISTIAN CHARITY
Seventeenth Century
ST VINCENT DE PAUL AND HIS HELPERS, 1576–1660

THE history of the Christian Church must be told, as all other histories are told, by describing its critical events and its great men, the establishing of its creeds and its government, its expansion among the nations, and its battles against evil in the world and within itself. But while the names of popes and councils, bishops and reformers stand out with especial clearness, it must be remembered that the history of the Church is also the history of the millions of ordinary men and women who, among all the troubles and changes that went on around them, practised their faith. They worshipped as they believed their Lord had commanded them, heard and considered the Scriptures, tried to share their faith with heathen neighbours, and helped their neighbours in sickness, need and distress, in the spirit of the Good Samaritan.

Christians had been noted for their works of charity and mercy ever since the Church was founded. Bishops, like Basil, founded hospitals and tended the plague-stricken, the Church of the Middle Ages cared for the lepers, the early monasteries fed and sheltered the destitute, and the noble almshouses of later days were built and endowed by wealthy Christian folk, whilst the gifts and services of nameless poorer people never ceased. From the Middle Ages onwards there had been little groups of Christians who had formed Brotherhoods or Confraternities, binding themselves to rules of prayer and works of charity, and it was largely because of such people, together with noble ladies, citizens, workmen, and peasants, that Vincent de Paul was able to do his great work for the suffering poor of France in the seventeenth century.

In these times the condition of the poor in Europe was terrible. A war, arising partly out of the quarrels between Catholics and Protestants, wasted Germany for thirty years, and in France there were battles and massacres and assassinations, armies belonging to this party and that went through the country plundering and destroying the slow, hard labour of the peasants. Their harvests ruined and their homes burnt, many of the wretched peasants flocked into the cities to try to find work, or beg or steal, whilst others lived, half-starved, in the villages.

They were starved in mind and soul as well

as in body, for few of the clergy cared for them. The Roman Catholic Church in France was in a bad way; the title and wealth that went with bishoprics and abbacies was still often given to people who never intended to do the work themselves, but put careless, ignorant and badly-paid men in their places. Yet, as in all bad times, there were some good men, bishops and priests, who fought against these evils, and among them one of the greatest and best was Vincent de Paul. This priest, who had been a peasant himself, began his work in a house in Paris, where he trained other priests [1] as missioners, taught them to preach simply and clearly, and sent them out to the peasantry of the French villages. In Paris he inspired a group of French ladies (his " Ladies of Charity ") to take food and comforts to the sick poor in the great hospitals of the city, and to adopt and provide for many of the foundling babies who had been deserted by mothers too poor to feed them. But work was needed among the village women which these high-born ladies of Paris could not do, and it was Madame le Gras, the wife of a court secretary, who first thought of banding together the rough peasant girls of the countryside to do it. So the Order of the Sisters of Charity was founded, a little group who, in

---

[1] They came to be called Lazarists, because their house was named St Lazare (Lazarus).

their coarse blue dresses and white caps, went out to nurse and serve the poor, and who found no work too hard or horrible or dangerous to do. Two of them were sent out to nurse the starving, dying people of Arras after a siege, and four to the hospitals of Calais, where six hundred French were lying wounded after a battle with Spain. Of these, two died of overwork and the infection, but when Vincent read to those in Paris the report of what had happened, there was a rush of volunteers to fill their places. It was grim work, but the mission priests had worse things to face. One of the most dreadful effects of civil war was the disease which came from the bodies of dead men and horses left unburied. The courageous priests had not hesitated to cross tracts of country full of lawless, plundering soldiers as they carried food to the famine-stricken areas, nor did they hesitate to deal with this far more dangerous work— they took up their spades and buried the dead. Some of them died at their posts, "truly martyrs" their leader said, but they must have saved hundreds of lives.

Vincent de Paul had the gift of calling men and women to do great things in the name of Christ. He sent help to the wretched galley slaves at the ports, he organised a scheme for ransoming Christian travellers whose ships had been seized by the Turks and who were being sold [1] as slaves in the market of Algiers, and he sent missionaries out to the deadly climate of the island of Madagascar. Those who obeyed him knew that they had a leader who was utterly fearless and never spared himself. When Paris rose against the Queen and an army was sent to besiege and starve the city, this old man of seventy-three rode his horse through the dark city streets one night, across the flooded Seine Bridge, and straight to St Germain's, to beg her for help. The Queen let some corn get through to the people of Paris, but she would not stop the war. Through all the terrible time when the rebellion was being crushed, Vincent went on with the work of teaching and relieving distress, and when he died his helpers still carried on. When, in later times, France banished the Religious Orders, they had to go too, but they carried on their work elsewhere. In England we can still see the Sisters of Charity in blue dresses and white caps such as the first peasant girls wore, going about to nurse the sick and help the poor and care for the foundlings, as they did in France three hundred years ago.

[1] This had happened to Vincent de Paul when he was young.

NOTES   .   .   .   .

OTHER GREAT FRENCH CHURCHMEN of the sixteenth and seventeenth centuries were FRANCIS OF SALES, the wise and kind Bishop of Geneva ; BOSSUET, Bishop of Meaux ; the famous preacher, FENELON, Archbishop of Cambrai, and MADAM GUYON,[1] who practised and taught a quiet, simple way of prayer ; AGNES ARNAULD, who reformed the Benedictine convent at Port-Royal ; and BLAISE PASCAL, the thinker and writer.

RELIGION IN THE EIGHTEENTH CENTURY.—By this time the dreadful wars between Catholics and Protestants were over, and the most savage persecutions had ceased, though no Protestants might gather for worship in France, and Roman Catholics were denied legal rights in England. But the world was tired and bitter and afraid of any sort of religious enthusiasm, lest it should bring back these evils. This was especially true of England, where most of the rich and intellectual people openly despised Christianity, and the poor, to whom no one preached, were drunken and lawless. Churchmen and Dissenters tried to suppress the ruffians of the towns by co-operating

[1] Some of her teaching was condemned by the Pope because it was believed to discourage people from other important ways of prayer, especially Confession and Communion. This had been the result of the teaching of a Spaniard named MOLINOS, whose method came to be called Quietism.

with the police, but they failed. In the country, especially in the districts where the coal-mining industry was developing, great numbers of people, degraded by toil and poverty and neglect, had become practically heathen again. Yet in these darkest times there broke out what has been known ever since as THE EVANGELICAL [1] REVIVAL, and its leader was JOHN WESLEY.

[1] "Evangelize" comes from a Greek word which means, "I bring good news." Wesley and those who worked with him were called Evangelicals because they preached the Good News of the New Testament.

CHAPTER XXIV

THE EVANGELICAL REVIVAL
Eighteenth Century

JOHN WESLEY, 1703–1791

AMONG the clergy of the English Church there were some, like Vincent de Paul, who were living out the Faith they professed, keeping the rules of the Church, and doing their best to help the poor around them.

At Christchurch College, Oxford, in the year 1730, a group of men had banded themselves together for this purpose. They went to the services in the college chapels, made their Communion every week, kept the Church fasts, visited and helped the sick and poor and those in prison. Their companions laughed at them, and nicknamed them The Holy Club, and some called them *Methodists*. Among these men there was George Whitefield, the son of an innkeeper, and two sons of a Lincolnshire clergyman, Charles Wesley, and his brother John, who became their leader. These three men were ordained in the English Church, they went out to work in the newly founded colony of Georgia, and returned

194

to wake the people of England out of their dull carelessness, and change the spirit of the whole country.

John Wesley had met some German Protestants (Moravians) on his travels, and after he came back to England it was at one of their meetings that a great religious experience came to him, changing his whole life.   Up to this time he had preached what he believed to be true, that God loved men and that Christ had died for them ; but now he *felt* it to be true about himself, and he was filled with a great longing to preach it to everyone. He had no church of his own, so he preached wherever anyone would lend him a pulpit, and he and others like him sometimes gathered together for great prayer-meetings which went on far into the night.   Some bishops and priests were kind and friendly to John Wesley, others suspected and disliked him, and were afraid of the excitement that followed his sermons.   They disliked George Whitefield more, because of his strong Calvinistic views and his even more exciting sermons.

It was the fact that he was often forbidden to preach in churches, and the sight of the great crowds that waited to hear him, that made Whitefield decide that he would preach in the open air, and Wesley followed his example.   It seems strange to us that this should have shocked people, for the friars had always done it. But during the times of persecution, when preaching had been forbidden except in the Established Church, people had grown to be afraid of any big gatherings of this sort. So Whitefield and Wesley and their followers were mobbed and stoned, their meetings broken up, their listeners attacked. Some people thought of them as Dissenters (who were still suspected and disliked), others believed them to be Jesuits, and some held that they were trying to bring back the Pretender to England. Often it was ignorant mobs that attacked them, sometimes it was magistrates who sent to arrest them, and sometimes the clergy of the English Church stirred up the people against them. But nothing daunted these evangelists. Whitefield preached wherever he could get a crowd : from a tombstone in the churchyard, from a scaffold at a public execution, from the platform of a puppet show at a fair. Great crowds of colliers at Kingswood, near Bristol, gathered to hear him, and he tells how the tears made white gutters on their sooty faces as they sobbed with emotion at his words. So, too, John Wesley preached, though more calmly, yet he knew what it was to have his congregation crying and groaning round him. The Methodists talked straight to the hearts of the people ; they made each one feel that God cared for him, that Christ had died for him, and that his soul mattered more than anything else in the world. Many of the poorer people had never been inside the dull, respectable parish churches of their day, and no one had ever spoken to them like this. It was little wonder that they were so moved. But Wesley could preach another sort of sermon when he faced a crowd of careless, curious listeners, and then his burning words on the wrath of God against their cold, evil ways would often startle them into fear and repentance.

Up and down the English countryside he rode, a small, neatly dressed figure, with a quiet, rosy face and long hair that curled at the ends. Over the flat fen country he went to preach at his father's old church at Epworth, but the vicar refused to let him, so he stood on his father's tomb in the churchyard and held a great crowd spell-bound for hours. He rode through the green dales and heathery hills of Yorkshire to the old town of Whitby, where the simple fisher-folk loved him and listened to him. He spoke to fashionable crowds in the city of Bath. At Walsall a roaring mob swept him down the main street, and it seemed as if his last hour had come. In the depths of winter he would be up at five in the morning and preaching to the people of Devonshire, then riding àcross the snow-covered moors of Cornwall in a hailstorm to an evening meeting at Gwennap Pit. Once he escaped from his enemies by sailing from one Cornish cove to another. These are only a few of the stories that are told to us in the thrilling *Journal* that he wrote. He went from end to end of England, to Ireland, to Scotland, to Wales, to Holland.

When John Wesley preached he hoped that his hearers would feel, as he had felt, the joyful assurance of forgiveness and new life. But he knew that this feeling must work itself out in a good life, and wherever he went he organised little classes of people who were to meet every week to pray and help each other to live like Christians, giving what money they could spare to help those who were in need or distress. Wesley himself was always trying to help the poor, and, even when he was an old man of eighty-two, we read of him tramping ankle-deep in the slushy London snow, begging money to buy warm clothes for those who had none.

In the great work which he did he needed many helpers, and, as there were not enough clergy in sympathy with him, he arranged that some of the work should be done by lay-preachers, whose courage and self-sacrifice were nearly as great as his own. Wesley had always declared that he was loyal to the Church of England ; he would not hold his meetings at the same time as the Sunday services, and he always told his followers to make their Communion at their own parish church. But when he could not continue his work without more clergy, he put into practice his idea that priest and bishop are one person, and that any priest can ordain others. By ordaining men himself—which was contrary to the belief and practice of the Church of England—he made the Methodists a separate denomination.

NOTES . . . .

THE WESLEYAN METHODISTS.—These Churches are divided into circuits and districts, the ministers of each circuit meet quarterly, and a Conference of all the Churches meets once a year. Their ministers only stay in one church for a few years and then move on; they are still travelling evangelists, as they were in Wesley's time, and there are still lay-preachers and class meetings. In America the Church is called Episcopal because its superintendents are called Bishops.[1]

After Wesley died several groups of Methodists broke away from the main body, some because they thought that lay people ought to have more responsibility in the Church, and others because they wanted more open-air preaching and revival meetings. One of these groups called themselves the PRIMITIVE METHODISTS, whose leaders,

[1] The first Methodist "bishop" was ordained by Wesley: his name was Coke.

HUGH BOURNE and WILLIAM CLOWES, were famous evangelists of their times.

THE CALVINISTIC METHODISTS.—John Wesley disagreed with Whitefield's Calvinistic views, and their followers separated. Whitefield's followers came to be called the CALVINISTIC METHODISTS ; they were very much helped by SELINA, COUNTESS OF HUNTINGDON, and two of their best-known preachers, HOWELL HARRIS and DANIEL ROW-LANDS, evangelised Wales.

THE INFLUENCE OF THE REVIVAL was seen in the change which took place in the character and habits of the English people. Everyone began to take life more seriously, to care more about religion, purity, and honour, and about the condition of the poor and oppressed. It was seen in the lives of the English clergy, like HENRY VENN of Clapham, and THOMAS SCOTT, FLETCHER of Madeley, and of WILLIAM COWPER, the poet and hymn-writer. In 1781 ROBERT RAIKES founded the first Sunday schools, and in the next century ELIZABETH FRY worked unceasingly for the reform of the horrible gaols of England and Europe.

One of Wesley's last letters was written to William Wilberforce, urging him to fight " that execrable villainy," the slave trade. Whitefield and many of the English clergy saw nothing wrong in owning slaves, but the Society of Friends had already protested against it, and forbidden

their members to have anything to do with it
(1761). In America JOHN WOOLMAN (1728-1772)
testified quietly and bravely against its cruelty,
and another Friend, LEVI COFFIN (1798-1877),
helped hunted slaves to escape into those States
where they were safe. The lonely death of JOHN
SMITH (1790-1824), friend of the slaves in Deme-
rara, and the courageous words of WILLIAM
KNIBB, Baptist missionary to Jamaica, helped to
carry the victory, and in 1833 an Act of Parliament
set free all slaves in the British Empire.

HYMN SINGING.—The crowds that gathered to
hear the preachers of the Great Revival expressed
their joy and enthusiasm in hymns. Some of
these (*Our God, our help in ages past*) had been
written by a Congregationalist minister, ISAAC
WATTS (1674-1748); one famous hymn (*Rock of
Ages*) by AUGUSTUS TOPLADY, a follower of Whitefield; but the greatest number of them were made
by Charles Wesley, who wrote *Jesus, Lover of my
Soul*. These hymns, like the great songs men
always sing when they feel deeply—battle songs,
songs of triumph, love songs—were full of feeling
and set to strong, swinging tunes.

But the hymns of the Christian faith which had
been written by the Churchmen of ancient times
and by the men of the Middle Ages, were unknown
to the Methodists. Many of them had never
been translated from the Latin and Greek in which

they were written. They came to be loved and sung by men who fought as nobly for the glory and honour of the Church as had the leaders of the Evangelical Revival. These men were called " Tractarians," and one of the first of them was JOHN KEBLE. Their later followers became known as ANGLO-CATHOLICS.

CHAPTER XXV

THE ANGLO-CATHOLIC REVIVAL

NINETEENTH CENTURY

JOHN KEBLE, 1792-1866; JOHN MASON NEALE, 1818-1866

JUST as the revivalists had stirred up the people of England to feel and practise the religion they believed, so the Tractarians stirred them up to realise the meaning of Churchmanship, to restore the beauty and dignity of English Church worship and its discipline, and to see it as part of the great Catholic Church of East and West, now represented by Roman, Orthodox, and Anglican.

From the sixteenth century onwards there had always been men who emphasised the fact that the English Church had never become Protestant or Reformed as had that of the followers of Luther, Calvin, or Zwingli. Archbishop Laud was one of them, Bishop Jeremy Taylor, who wrote a famous book called *Holy Living and Holy Dying*, was another, and there were many among the Non-Jurors. (One of the Non-Jurors was William Law, a priest who befriended John Wesley when he was young, and tried to reform the careless and worldly people of his time by a book called

A Serious Call to a Devout and Holy Life).   But after
the Non-Juring bishops had been deprived of
their Sees, those who were left in power allowed
the Church to be subjected to the State[1] in such
a way that it seemed as if it would disappear al-
together.   *Convocation*, the assembly through which
the Church expressed itself, was not allowed to
meet, and by the nineteenth century things were
in a very bad way.   People thought of the Church
of England as a department of the State, and
though there were a few good men doing fine
work, many of its services were conducted in a
dull and slovenly way in dirty uncared-for buildings, where people rarely made their communion
more than once or twice a year.   In these dark
times a handful of great men rose up to help
and defend the Church.   Their names were John
Keble, Hurrell Froude, John Henry Newman, and
Edward Pusey.

In the year 1833, when Parliament had taken
upon itself to abolish some bishoprics in Ireland,
John Keble, Fellow and Tutor of Oriel College,
Oxford, preached a sermon which was a trumpet-
call to his fellows to stand up for the rights of
the Church.   His sympathisers gathered round him,

[1] A great deal of power had been given to the King since the
days of Henry VIII, but the King was a member of the Church,
bound to obey its laws and defend it.   Parliament, which came
to govern instead of the King, was by 1829 composed of men
who might have any belief or none.

and they began to issue great numbers of penny and twopenny tracts (from which they got their name, Tractarians). Most of these tracts were written by Newman, then the Vicar of St Mary's Church, Oxford, and a famous writer and preacher. There was a great storm of opposition, and it grew worse when Newman and others joined the Roman Catholic Church. But the rest of the Tractarians stood firm. They made it possible for people to study Church history by editing and translating the works of the early Fathers of the Church and the writers of the seventeenth century; they tried to make friends with the other branches of the Catholic Church, and by their own real and splendid goodness they brought many people to their way of thinking.

Keble's life from 1836 onwards was that of a parish priest in a Hampshire village, where he lived translating and visiting and serving the people of the countryside. There was a service every day in Keble's church, and he taught in the village school, and prepared the children for confirmation. He took endless pains over them, and if any of them lived too far away to come to him when their day's work was done, he would set off for their cottages with a lantern and teach them there. He visited his sick people conscientiously, half his income went to help the poor, and he preached sermons which the most ignorant of them could understand. Though he was a Professor of Poetry [1] and a famous writer, he was so humble that many of his people never knew he was a famous man, and the children were quite surprised when the village schoolmistress told them that Mr Keble was much cleverer than she was !

While Keble was working in his parish, another Tractarian priest, John Mason Neale, was also trying to make the rather narrow-minded and ignorant people of his time realise the glory and splendour of the whole Catholic Church in all the ages, and feel proud that they belonged to it. He did this by translating old Greek and Latin prayers and hymns, and the Liturgies of the Eastern Church, by writing Church history and stories of the saints of all centuries. He wrote many of these stories for children, and he made the people in his stories seem so real and alive that one child said, " How old Mr Neale must be to have talked to so many saints and martyrs ! " Some of the clergy of the Orthodox Church were very grateful to Neale for helping the people of the West to understand them, and the Czar of Russia sent him a hundred pounds for his work. Neale translated into English some of the finest hymns that are now in our hymn books, old hymns which tell of the central things of the Christian faith in strong,

[1] Keble wrote a book of poetry called *The Christian Year*.

simple, dignified language, such as *The Royal Banners forward go* and *Jerusalem the golden*. He wrote some hymns himself as well as translating, among them, *O happy band of pilgrims* and the lovely Christmas carol, *Good King Wenceslas*. During the greater part of his life Neale was Warden of Sackville College at East Grinstead, an almshouse and church built in 1608 for the support of sixty poor old people. He found it in a very bad condition, and he did a lot to make the old people comfortable and happy. He made the church beautiful, and on Sundays and festivals, after he had celebrated the Eucharist, they used to dine with him. Festivals were real feasts when Neale was there, and there were plum puddings and mince pies at Christmas! Besides all this he founded the Sisterhood of St Margaret, a band of women who gave themselves up to a life of prayer and service for the sick poor, very much as St Vincent's Sisters did. We get some idea of the heroism of these women when we read that they went to nurse a case of typhus and found that the patient had not been tended for a whole week, and that people were too frightened to go to the house even to bring them water from the river near by!

Neale helped to found a society for the preserving and restoring of old churches and the building of new ones in which Christian worship

could be conducted in an atmosphere of beauty.
The early Tractarians had set out to teach people
Catholic principles ; the later ones began to
express that teaching in worship.   Once more the
Eucharist was celebrated with joyful and splendid
ceremony, the candles were lit, and the priest
wore the vestments of the Catholic Church (see
p. 210).   These men were not always wise in
what they did.   They sometimes copied the ways
of the Roman Church, when they might just as
well have used good Catholic customs that were
English, and they sometimes offended good people
by not explaining carefully and patiently what
they meant and were trying to do.   So ignorant
people thought that Roman Catholicism and the
Inquisition were going to be established in England, and the opponents of the Tractarians tried
every method of crushing them.   There were
riots and law-suits.   Mobs shouted outside during
services and threw stones at the windows ; spies
and informers, pretending to worship, carried
away tales of what was done; and Neale's poor
old men at Sackville College were worried and
confused by questions and warnings.   Tractarians were fined, prevented from doing their
work, and some went to prison.   But they went
on saying and doing what they believed to be
right, and they steadily influenced the English
Church.   People could not help feeling that the

Tractarians were a finer set of men than most of their enemies. They grew to respect conscientious parish priests like Keble, kindly great-minded scholars like Neale, and courageous vicars in slum parishes like Charles Lowder, who stopped street-fights, faced angry mobs, and carried cholera victims to the hospital in his arms.

So the great change began; worship became more frequent and more reverent, artists and craftsmen once more joined forces to make the church beautiful, the best of the old music and hymns and prayers were used and some good new ones written. Old Church customs were studied, and some of them revived. Men as well as women began to dedicate themselves to a life of prayer and works of charity or education, as the monks and nuns had done long ago.[1] Best of all, though all that the Tractarians stood for was not accepted by the rest of the Church, yet from that time onwards the Church of England began to assert its true rights, and to teach its members that the first duty of Christian people is to their Lord and the Body which He has commissioned to carry on His work.

[1] A Sisterhood was begun by Pusey in 1845, and the Society of St John the Evangelist for men in 1866.

NOTES . . . .

VESTMENTS AND CHURCH COLOURS.—When the people of the Roman Empire came to adopt the coat and trousers which the barbarians wore, the clergy still kept the graceful dress of the old world: a long-sleeved robe with girdle, a cloak, and a scarf of office, and these have been worn at the Eucharist in Catholic churches ever since.[1] In the West the robe of white linen is called an *Alb*, the cloak is either a *Cope*, a *Chasuble*, or a *Dalmatic*, according to its shape and use, the scarf a *Stole*. These vestments naturally came to suggest that those who wore them accepted the Catholic view of the Eucharist, so the Reformed Churches discarded them and wore a doctor's black gown, and the Friends wore their ordinary clothes. There was a great deal of controversy about the vestments in the English Church, and a compromise was reached, but the Tractarians revived the old Catholic dress, and it is used to-day in very many churches.

At first the vestments and church hangings were of no special colours, though the most beautiful were used for festivals, and this is the case in the East to-day. But in the West symbo-

---

[1] There are two other vestments, an AMICE, which may have been a neckcloth, and the MANIPLE, which may have been a handkerchief.

lical colours began to be used for the seasons—blue or violet for Advent, purple or ash-colour for Lent, purple or red and black for Passiontide, white or gold for the great festivals (Christmas, Easter, Ascension, Trinity, All Saints, Michaelmas, etc.), red for Whitsuntide and the feasts of martyrs, and green for the times when there is no special feast or fast.

THE REVIVAL OF THE MISSIONARY SPIRIT.—The great revivals of religion which had occurred in other lands as well as in England in the eighteenth and nineteenth centuries, made men and women want to share the joy of being a Christian with the rest of the world. Up to this time the Faith had spread mainly :

(1) In the first and second centuries, through the Apostles and early Christian travellers and traders.

(2) In the fourth and fifth centuries, through the travels and exiles of some of the great bishops.[1]

(3) From the fourth to the tenth century, through the monks.

(4) In the thirteenth and following centuries, through the Friars.

[1] Two famous missionary bishops, Ulphilas the West Goth (313-383), and Nestorius (?-450), held some views which were condemned by the Catholic Church. Nevertheless, they taught a great deal of the true faith, and Ulphilas translated the Scriptures.

(5) In the sixteenth and following centuries, through the Jesuits.

(6) In the sixteenth and following centuries, through the colonists and settlers and their chaplains in the New World and other territories.

Though there had been some splendid missionaries during the Middle Ages and the Renaissance, much of the work they did failed. Many of them worked far too fast and did not learn the language of the natives, nor their ways of thinking, nor translate the Bible for them. The quarrels between the Friars and the Jesuits, and the bad lives of some colonists and settlers, brought disgrace on the Christian name. Moreover, the first missionaries were often followed by armed adventurers who seized the land and ill-treated or enslaved the people, and they came to be distrusted because they belonged to the conquering race.

In 1732 the Moravians sent out their first missionary to the negroes of the Dutch East Indies. It was the beginning of a great enterprise which has never ceased, for the Moravians have sent out more missionaries in proportion to their size than any other part of the Christian Church.

Some of the finest missionary work was done :

(7) In the eighteenth and nineteenth centuries by the Missionary Societies.

England already had a SOCIETY FOR THE PROMOTION OF CHRISTIAN KNOWLEDGE (1689), and in 1701 a SOCIETY FOR THE PROPAGATION OF THE GOSPEL was established. This was followed by the formation of societies by the Baptists, Congregationalists, Church of England (C.M.S.), the Methodists, and the Churches of Scotland. Germany and Scandinavia were among the first to form societies, America began in 1810, the French Protestants later, and a Roman Catholic Missionary Society among the working girls of the silk mills at Lyons (The Society for the Propagation of the Faith). The Russian Church evangelised East Prussia and Siberia through JOHN VENIANIMOFF, MACARIUS, and NICOLAI IVANOWITCH ILMINSKY. The British and Foreign Bible Society, which was founded in 1804, was of great service to the missionaries.

The missionaries of the nineteenth century had to face the difficulties of unknown and even unwritten languages, the hostility of savage peoples and of the great trading societies, yet they went out into all the five continents and to the far isles of the Pacific, and their names are so many that even some of the greatest of them cannot be mentioned here.

CHAPTER XXVI

THE WORLD FOR CHRIST
Nineteenth Century

WILLIAM CAREY, 1761–1834 ; ROBERT MORRISON, 1782–1834 ;
JOHN WILLIAMS, 1795–1839 ; ALEXANDER MACKAY,
1849–1890

From Germany and Scandinavia, France and
Holland, America and England, the famous missionaries of these times made their way into every
known country of the world. It is a great story,
and, in spite of some mistakes and failures, they
did wonderful things. Before the century opened
the London Missionary Society had crossed the
world and brought the Gospel to the people of
the eastern South Sea Islands, and in 1841 an
English bishop of New Zealand was heroically
at work in a diocese of 96,000 sq. miles. Bishop
Selwyn called Coleridge Patteson from England
to help him, and Patteson became Bishop of the
Western Islands and died a martyr's death at the
hands of those who mistook him for one of the
slave seizers   China opened its ports to foreign
trade in 1842, and the missionaries entered immediately, Americans first, following in the steps
of the pioneers who had dared to enter and work

at the risk of their lives.   Fifty years later, when
the anti-foreign feeling took the shape of a terrible
massacre of Christians,[1] Chinese men and women
had so learned their Faith that they gave up their
lives willingly rather than deny it.   In 1859 the
closed country of Japan permitted foreigners to
enter its ports, closed for over two centuries, since
a great massacre of native Christians had taken
place, and Christianity had been forbidden on
pain of death.   The Roman Catholics were in
first, and they found there villagers who had
secretly practised the Faith as well as they could
remember it during the whole of that time.   Many
of these Christians were put to death on proclaiming that they were Christians, but fourteen years
later toleration was established.   But before the
ports were opened, a missionary-hearted priest of
the Orthodox Church had settled in Japan and
begun his work in secret, Father Nicolai, who
afterwards became a bishop.   Through the help
of the Russian Christians, but chiefly through the
Japanese Christians, a cathedral of the Orthodox
Church was built in Tokio.

In India the Danish Lutherans were the first to
begin missionary work; Carey, the Baptist, was
the first English pioneer, Henry Martyn worked
for six tremendous years translating the New
Testament into Hindustani and Persian, and

The Boxer Rising, 1900.

Alexander Duff, of the Church of Scotland, established schools for advanced education among the high-caste Hindus.

Missionaries had entered South Africa some time before the great pioneer, David Livingstone, blazed a trail through the centre of the Dark Continent and called on his fellow Christians to follow him. They followed, and went farther, pioneering, evangelising, establishing schools and training centres, witnessing by a life of prayer and devotion to the reality of their God.

The missionaries were great civilisers, and in preaching the Gospel they taught men a hundred other good things.

Some were pioneers or explorers, opening up country to be made safe and healthy and fertile and fit to live in. Among these were David Livingstone and Mary Slessor in Africa, John Williams in the South Seas, Judson in Burma.

Others became great linguists and translators of the Scriptures : such were William Carey in India, Robert Morrison in China, Henry Martyn in Persia, Bishop Patteson in Melanesia, Veniaminoff in Serbia, and James Evans among the Red Indians.

Some were doctors, healing the people, stopping the ravages of plague, and studying tropical diseases at great risk to themselves : of this profession was Pennell of Afghanistan. Others served hospitals, nursed the sick, and even became lepers (as Father Damien of Molokai did) in trying to help those wretched people.

There were those who gave themselves up to the work of schools—Alexander Duff and Miller of Madras ; or to industrial training centres, as Stewart of Lovedale in Africa, and Charles Abel in Papua ; and many of them served the cause of science by their observations in unknown countries.

The missionaries of these times came from all classes of society and all trades and professions.

Among the greatest was William Carey of Paulerspury, in Northamptonshire, once a cobbler, who bravely demanded of his fellow Baptists why Christians did not take the Gospel to the heathen. He was met with scorn and laughter at first, but he would not be silenced, answering the talk of risks and dangers with the words, " Expect great things from God, attempt great things for God." Thus the Baptist Missionary Society was founded in 1792 by a few poor men who offered twelve and a half guineas to it, and Carey offered himself to be its first missionary. With a colleague, John Thomas, he sailed to North India and began an almost desperate struggle to earn enough to support himself and his family, pick up the language, and get permission [1] to preach to people.

[1] India was not then part of the British Empire, and the trading companies which held land there did not like missions.

At last the Danish governor of Serampore invited them to settle there, helped them to build a church, and gave them permission to preach.   Here Carey, with his fellow missionaries Marshman and Ward, began his famous translation of the Bible, and set up printing presses.   Carey was a born linguist, and he had managed to learn Latin, Greek and Hebrew before he left England.   His fame spread.   He became not only a preacher and translator, but a teacher of Oriental languages in the Government College at Calcutta.   His influence spread far and wide.   One of his pupils was that great Englishman, John Lawrence of the Punjab.   His protests helped to stop the burning alive of Indian widows and the sacrifice of children.   From his printing press copies of the Scriptures went out to all parts of India.   He gave nearly all the money he earned to the cause of the mission, and died a poor man.   A University College at Serampore carries on his work.

Robert Morrison, another linguist, began learning Latin and Greek while he made his lasts, in order to prepare himself to go to college and train for the ministry.   There he thought and dreamed of the world's great need, and prayed, " Send me where workers are most wanted, send me to that part of the world where the difficulties are greatest."   He offered himself to the London Missionary Society, and they answered his prayer.

They sent him to a land whose language had forty-five thousand characters, and where any word said in a slightly different tone means something quite different; only one Englishman knew that language, and he was not in England. They sent him to a country that loathed foreigners, had turned out the Portuguese and the Dutch, and only tolerated the hated East India Company in two restricted areas. They sent him to the vast ancient empire of China, whose inhabitants had been highly civilised when the natives of Britain had been savages, and which no Protestant missionary had yet entered.

Morrison got a Chinaman to begin teaching him the language from two books made by Catholic missionaries. No English ship would take him to China, so he had to go to America and chance finding one there. The owner of the ship looked at him with an amused smile as he signed his papers. " And so, Mr Morrison, you really expect you will make an impression on the idolatry of the great Chinese Empire." " No," came the swift, stern answer, " but I expect God will." Morrison reached Canton, and lodged in a wretched little basement that had been part of a factory, in its suburbs. He learned more Chinese in secret, his teacher and himself in grave danger all the time, for it was thought a crime to teach the noble Chinese tongue to a despised barbarian

European! But the East India Company soon discovered his talent and employed him as a translator, and the work and the wage he earned helped him still further. He plodded away at his enormous, dangerous task. In ten years he had printed an Anglo-Chinese dictionary. In twelve, with the help of another translator, he had turned the whole Bible into Chinese. It was a foundation on which every Protestant missionary who followed him could build.

When Carey was in India, and Morrison in China, a young man named John Williams, who had been an ironmonger's assistant in City Road, London, sailed across the world with his nineteen-year-old wife to work for the London Missionary Society in the South Seas. From the Society Islands, where he taught the natives to read and write and build houses, he went to Rarotonga on a trading ship, and there dreamed of carrying the Gospel farther. He had no ship, so he built one! With a few tools, a derelict ship's cable, and the grass and trees of the island he built a seventy ton ship, her masts straight tree-trunks, her planks split from curved ones, her sails native matting, her anchor a crate of stones, and wooden nails to hold her together. In *The Messenger of Peace* he took the Gospel of Peace to warlike tribes, and more than once his words stopped the horrors of war. His last journey was to the Melanesian islands, whose fierce inhabitants had even turned away the brave explorer, Captain Cook. At the hands of these men John Williams met his death.

But " the blood of the martyrs is seed." Natives of Samoa and white men and women also laid down their lives for the island where he had been killed, and in the end Erromanga was won. The son of the man who murdered John Williams laid the foundation stone of a memorial to him.

Nearly forty years after Williams died a young engineer named Alexander Mackay began his work for the Church Missionary Society in the newly opened continent of Africa. He began by making a road from the coast to their mission station at Mpwapwa. " Our work is to spread the Gospel to the ends of the earth, and where we don't find a way we make it," he said.

He built the road and made his way to Uganda, north-west of the Victoria Lake. The story of that journey is a story of endless difficulties : untrained oxen, bad drivers, stinging flies, wild beasts, fierce suspicious savages, the loss of food, ammunition and medicines, the death of one companion, the murder of two others who had gone ahead, and the wreck of the boat he had brought on the shores of the lake. But he reached Uganda, and for a while held the favour of King Mtesa; translated the Gospel of St Matthew into his language ; taught the lazy, snobbish people that the followers of the Carpenter think it no shame to work with their hands; and baptised some of them in His name. A new heathen king drove him from the mission station; he settled in another, sent messages of help and comfort to Christians in Uganda, and died at his post. Those Christians were among the most heroic martyrs who have ever died for their Faith, and in the end Uganda was won, and from thence the Faith spread farther yet.

NOTES . . . .

CHRISTIANITY AND SOCIAL REFORM.—The revival of religion not only sent men to the far ends of the earth as foreign missionaries, it raised them up to fight the evils which were making heathens in their own country, and it filled them with a new sympathy for the poor, and a determination to overthrow the things which oppressed and enslaved them. In England there was a great deal of poverty and distress in country and town. The invention of machinery and the factory system at first created bad conditions of living and working. Men were crippled by accidents and exhausted by long hours of monotonous machine-work; women worked at heavy tasks and had no time to look after their homes; young children were employed in mills and mines sometimes for over twelve hours a day. Insanitary country cottages and bad houses hurriedly built near the factories, caused outbreaks of horrible disease, and there was no district nursing system. The majority of wealthy people were indifferent to what was happening, partly because they knew little about it, partly because most of them had lost the old idea that Christians are responsible for one another, and partly because they never thought of the poor as having the same feelings as themselves. In the old days the Catholic Church had recognised different classes of people, but taught that each class had its duties and rights, and was responsible to the others. It also laid down some wise and good rules about work. This does not mean that people always kept those rules ; there was greed and oppression and suffering then, as later, but there was definite Church teaching about these things. But at the Renaissance, when the old simple conditions of work gave way to the more complicated life of trading, some of these old rules were no use and no new ones were made.[1] Protestants insisted that everyone must think out what he believed to be right, but this was very difficult, and by the nineteenth century many

[1] Richard Baxter had tried to teach his fellows a better way of thinking in the seventeenth century, and the Society of Friends had from the first insisted that the rules of the Christian life applied to their whole life, and not to one part of it.

people had got into the habit of thinking that Church life and business life had nothing to do with each other, and were angry if the Church said anything about the latter. Something had to be done, first, to make them see the dreadful suffering and injustice round about them, and secondly, to reawaken the old ideal of mutual responsibility and co-operation. One of the people who did this was a Church of England clergyman named CHARLES KINGSLEY.

CHAPTER XXVII
CHRISTIAN FELLOWSHIP
NINETEENTH CENTURY
CHARLES KINGSLEY, 1819-1875

IN the year 1848 the misery and distress of the people was such that some of them determined to reform the Parliamentary system[1] by force, if they could not do it by persuasion. On 10th April a hundred thousand men were to meet on Kennington Common, march to Westminster, and compel Parliament to accept the People's Charter, which they had drawn up. The Government had its troops ready and enrolled special constables.

That morning the young rector of Eversley, in Hampshire, came up to town. "The poor fellows mean well, however misguided," he said to a friend. "It would be horrible if there were blood shed. I am going to Kennington Common to see what man can do. Will you go with me?"

At Waterloo Bridge these two men heard that the great gathering had been a failure, so they turned back and went to their other friends to

[1] In those days only privileged people had votes, so the poor could not state their grievances in Parliament. The Chartists demanded that everyone should have a vote.

talk about things. A week later eight of these men had formed a society to help masters and workmen, buyers and sellers, to co-operate for the good of everybody, acting in justice and friendship, and in the belief that this whole world belongs to God, and that men and women ought to work together according to His laws. They called themselves *Christian Socialists* and their leader was the Reverend Frederick Denison Maurice, a clergyman of the Church of England.

The Christian Socialists influenced public opinion by lecturing and speaking and writing tracts about the state of affairs in England. Charles Kingsley wrote novels and poems, and songs too. He had a wonderful power of description, and he wrote about the sufferings of the poor in such a way that people saw them as they really were. In his novel, *Alton Locke*, he described how women starved on the miserable wages paid to them for making fine clothes. In his famous song of *The Three Fishers* he pictured the dangerous life of the deep-sea fishermen and the suffering and despair of the wives who waited for ships that never came back. In *The Water Babies* (which he wrote for children) he made people realise what it must feel like to be a sweep's boy, climbing dark, hot chimneys for a living, and despised because of dirty clothes and sooty face.

Kingsley not only showed what the poor

suffered: he taught that most of their sufferings came because men broke the laws of God—laws of the body and of health, laws of the mind, and laws of the soul. He used to lecture a good deal about health and sanitation. In those days people were shocked if anyone talked about drains, and it took a good deal of courage to tell them, as Kingsley did, that their refusal to face facts was the cause of the bad housing and disease of their times. In Eversley he did things as well as talking. When diphtheria broke out he used to go about with a big bottle of throat-mixture under his arm, and teach everyone how to gargle. When he found a man suffering from fever in a room that had no ventilation, he bored holes in the wall to let in the air. In the sermons he preached, and the lectures and readings and cottage meetings, Kingsley taught his people to use their minds as God would have them do, never to be afraid of any truth, and to store memory and imagination with good and beautiful things. He knew a lot about geology and natural history, and he opened their eyes to see something of the wonder and order of God's world. So, too, in his sermons and writings he spoke of the laws of God concerning the soul, warning masters and workmen that no plans to make things better could succeed if they were based on selfishness or cheating or laziness or violence.

Thus Kingsley lived and taught, and when he died a great crowd of all sorts of people came to his funeral. There was a representative of the Prince of Wales, and the gipsies from Eversley Common, the squire and the village labourers, the bishop of the diocese and many Nonconformists, high officials from the colonies and members of the House of Commons. There were authors and publishers and huntsmen in scarlet coats, because he had always loved good sportsmen, and outside the churchyard gates there were horses and hounds, because he also loved all the creatures of God. They laid his body in the earth, but his spirit and influence found its way into the hearts of all kinds of people. Christian opinion got Acts of Parliament passed to guard the health of the public and improve the housing of the poor, and parish councils worked to make local conditions better. The clergy spoke out boldly against the evils of their times, and some of them formed a guild " to study in common how to apply the moral truths and principles of Christianity to the social and economic difficulties of the present time." There were many hard things to do, and many hard problems to solve, but the Church was awake and trying to do its duty.

NOTES . . . .

AFTER THE CHRISTIAN SOCIALISTS.—From this time onward other guilds and societies were formed by the clergy for the same purpose ; they studied the social conditions of their time, the ways of betterment that had been suggested or tried, and endeavoured to discover what Christians of their own time ought to do.

Some of these clergy were Evangelicals, others were Anglo-Catholics. Three of their most famous leaders were STEWART HEADLAM, CHARLES GORE (afterwards Bishop of Oxford), and CANON SCOTT HOLLAND. A Jesuit, CHARLES PLATER, began this sort of work among the Roman Catholics, and Dr CLIFFORD (Baptist) was one of the first great leaders among the Free Churches.

In 1911 all the guilds and societies which had been formed began to hold inter-denominational conferences on social work ; in 1924 a great Conference on Christian Politics, Economics, and Citizenship was held at Birmingham, when 1400 delegates, representing all kinds of Christian Churches, came from England and other nations. This Conference (which came to be called C.O.P.E.C.) published reports of the conclusions of its members, and roused people to more and better work. Anglicans and Nonconformists worked together to get a truly Christian settlement of the General Strike in 1926, and three years later a *Christian Social Council* was organised to help everyone (of any denomination) who was doing this kind of work.

As the different denominations worked together they were bound to discuss the Faith which united them and to realise the differences which divided them from each other, and this was one of the things which led the way to the conferences on reunion which are described later on.

OTHER CHRISTIAN PEOPLE besides Kingsley worked to help the poor and oppressed in the nineteenth century. There were poets like WILLIAM BLAKE and TOM HOOD, and MRS BROWNING, who wrote of their sufferings; and novelists, like CHARLES DICKENS, who made his readers feel that even the most degraded people were human beings and could be loved. There were legislators, like LORD SHAFTESBURY, who toiled for years to get the hours of work in factories reduced. And there were men and women who went into the darkest and most dangerous places in England to help and to save those who needed them. The greatest of these were WILLIAM and CATHERINE BOOTH of the SALVATION ARMY.

CHAPTER XXVIII

THE SALVATION ARMY

NINETEENTH AND TWENTIETH CENTURIES

WILLIAM BOOTH, 1829–1912;
CATHERINE BOOTH, 1829–1890

WILLIAM BOOTH really knew something about the poor, for as a boy he had worked in a pawnshop in Nottingham. When he became a Methodist preacher both he and his wife, Catherine, felt that God had called them to preach to the roughest and most degraded kind of people, who never went near any sort of church.

The Methodist Churches of the time were not doing this, and Booth could not get them to appoint him as an evangelist, nor could he do what he wanted as the minister of an ordinary church. It was this that made him come to London to work on his own lines, taking his wife and six little children with him. They lived at first on the sale of some of their books and pamphlets, the money they collected at their meetings, and the help of one or two wealthy friends, and they preached wherever they could find a crowd or borrow a pulpit.

Many people were shocked at first at the sight of a woman preaching, but Catherine Booth had a mind and a power that made them listen, and a heart that made everybody love her. William Booth had his faults, like most other people. He was sometimes rough and self-willed, and forgot that other people were doing work for the kingdom of God besides himself and his followers : but he was utterly sincere and very courageous, and he never spared himself in his great work of preaching the Gospel to the wildest and wickedest people of the slums of London.

He began his work by standing on a bit of waste ground near some public-houses in Mile End Road, a tall, black-bearded man, waving a Bible and an umbrella to attract attention, and trying to shout above the roar of the traffic. He preached in an old stable ; he preached in a carpenter's shop near a pig-sty ; he preached in a ramshackle tent which let in the rain. It was a hard struggle at first, but at last they were able to hire public buildings for their meetings, and they gathered around them a band of loyal helpers which was called " The Salvation Army." It was organised on military lines, had flags and uniforms, and its officers and members were called captains, soldiers, etc. Booth was General.

William and Catherine Booth believed that everyone, however bad, could repent of his past and be saved by the power of God, beginning at once to lead a new life. When they preached they called people to come out to the " penitent form " and give themselves to Jesus Christ; and at these meetings wonderful things happened. Men and women who had been drunkards all their lives—cruel, unclean, sullen—rose up from where they had knelt, utterly changed : full of joy, and eager to share their new happiness with their comrades. General Booth organised his converts, men and women, into little companies and sent them out to save others. They went out into the streets and the worst of the slums, and told their story, prayed, sang hymns, and sometimes preached. They lived a self-denying life, did not touch drink [1] or tobacco, and dressed in the plainest clothes when they were not in the Army uniform.

It was a life of continual danger and adventure. Salvationists were mobbed and struck and pelted with rotten eggs and cabbage stalks and bad fish ; they were fined and taken to prison for making a disturbance in the streets (though it was their enemies who made the disturbance). Respectable people hated the noise they made and the strange, wild things they did to attract attention ; the jolly, rowdy hymns they sang ; and their blue and red and gold flag on which was written, " Blood and

[1] Many of these converts had been drunkards and drink would have been a temptation to them.

Fire." They did not realise that this was the Salvationist's way of saying that the Lord had shed His blood, and the Holy Ghost sent His fire, to save the people of England from the horrible drunkenness and cruelty and impurity and cold, narrow selfishness of the times, and that the poor understood this way of saying things.

The Salvationists were determined to make people hear their message, or die in the attempt, and they did not care how silly they looked if only they could attract attention. They banged tambourines and drums, and waved umbrellas ; they went wherever there was a crowd, or they made one. One man went and lay down silently in the snow in a public place for three-quarters of an hour every day for a week, and at the end of the week he had a crowd round him that felt he must have something to say that was worth hearing.

Among the first. heroic officers of the Salvation Army there were George Railton, a Methodist preacher ; Elijah Cadman, who had been a drunken chimney-sweep ; James Dowdle, a tall railway-guard who could play the fiddle ; and John Lawley.

Although the Salvationists were willing to starve and suffer for the cause of Christ, they determined to save others from starving and suffering because no one cared for them. For a time the Army ran cheap food shops, later they built shelters for the homeless, and homes for men and women and children who were in need or distress or unable to work. They organised labour exchanges, they helped discharged prisoners and the unemployed, some of whom they sent out to the colonies. But their first work was to change men's hearts and lives, and they did not believe that social work could succeed unless that was done.

The Salvationists went to Canada and Australia and America and France and Switzerland and India. After his wife died, brave to the last, and urging the Army on to greater things, General Booth travelled through the Continent and America, preaching and telling the story of his work. The courage and self-sacrifice of these men and women, and the wonderful things they did, had begun to win the respect and admiration of all sorts of people, and when the General died they united to honour him. Sixty-five thousand people marched past his coffin (over which hung his wife's portrait); the King and Queen, the German Emperor, and the American Ambassador sent wreaths for his grave. The daily papers, which had once ridiculed him, expressed their deep sorrow for his death. But the common men and women of the Army did him the greatest honour. They blew big trumpets and waved banners and sang triumphant hymns, because, as

they said, he had been " promoted to Glory."
A new General, his son, Bramwell Booth, took his
place, and the Army went marching on.

NOTES . . . .

SALVATION ARMY CEREMONIES.—When the
Army was first organised some of its members
were baptised people who made their Communion
in their own churches. Later the Army had its
special rules. Like the Society of Friends, and
unlike the other Christian Churches, the Salvationists do not believe the use of the Sacraments
to be the will and command of Christ. They feel
that the use of them may lead people to believe
that they can be saved merely by taking part in
a ceremony instead of by a changed life. However, they use many symbols (flags, uniforms, etc.),
and provide services for the dedication of children
to God, the renewal of vows of consecration, the
blessing of colours, and the celebration of wed-
dings and funerals, which their members may, and
generally do, use. They do not think that Christians should mourn at funerals, so they wear white
ribbons instead of black, and sing triumphant
hymns, believing that by death a Christian passes
to higher and happier service.

OTHER HELPERS OF THE POOR in these days
were the REVEREND WILSON CARLILE, who founded

the Church Army; Dr Barnardo, who provided homes for destitute children; and many temperance workers, who fought against the drunkenness of the times.

Christians of other Nations.—One of the first things the Salvationists did in foreign lands was to train those who followed their teaching to become leaders and officers, and to send them to preach to their own people. This is the aim of all missionaries, for no nation can thoroughly understand and express the Christian faith till it has leaders and teachers of its own race. In the early centuries the Eastern and Irish and Roman missionaries made converts of the British, and these men and women became leaders and teachers and built up the Christian civilisation of Britain in their own way. So also in the nineteenth and twentieth centuries the European missionaries made Christians among all other nations, and since then these have begun to take positions of importance in the Churches of their own countries.

CHAPTER XXIX

" THE NATIONS SHALL BRING THEIR GLORY "

Nineteenth and Twentieth Centuries

JAMES EMMAN KWEGYIR AGGREY, 1875–1927

WHEN the European missionaries of the nineteenth century went into all parts of the world, the civilisation which went with them and followed them carried evil as well as good along with it. It brought strong drink, and new and fatal diseases, encouraged the sale of opium, and introduced bad labour conditions along with machinery and the factory system. Moreover, when the non-Christian peoples gave up their old religion, they often gave up much that was wise and beautiful in their ancient art and literature, and some good and sensible ways of living and dressing [1] and working. In place of these they sometimes adopted European customs which were either bad or unsuited to their character and the climate of their country.

[1] The wearing of too many clothes had a bad effect on the health of people who were not used to them. Mrs John Williams made Victorian bonnets for the South Sea Islanders !

The wisest of the missionaries and their converts soon realised this, and began to try to withstand these evil influences, and to establish a Christian worship and civilisation which included the best of the old ways of the people of the land. Churches began to be built as nearly as possible in the style of native buildings, many of the old industries, songs, dances, and games were revived, and some schools [1] were organised on the native plan of living. As converts were trained to be priests and preachers, and Indians, Chinese, Japanese and Africans became bishops in the Episcopal churches, they were able to express the Christian faith, not only in the language of their own people, but in their own especial manner of thinking. Sometimes Christians adopted a method of living which was peculiar to their own countrymen, in order to preach the Gospel to them in the way they would best understand. So in India, Sundar Singh, a Christian Sikh of the Punjab, trained at the Divinity College at Lahore, decided that he could influence his people better if he were not ordained as a priest but went about as an Indian *Sadhu* or Holy Man. He travelled thus through his own country, with bare feet and a saffron robe, carrying only a Bible, a blanket, and a begging bowl, and became a great power for

[1] The Girls' School at Mbereshi, in Africa, is carried on on these lines.

good, both in India and other lands. Other Christians gave their lives to fighting the evils that were due to Western influence. In Africa Chief Khama succeeded in stopping the trade in strong drink within his territory. In China [1] Pastor Hsi invented pills that relieved the craving for opium, and worked with medicine and prayer and the power of a holy life to redeem the drug addicts among his people In Japan Toyohiko Kagawa worked, and still works, fighting bad labour conditions and slum housing. [2]

Sometimes this growing sense of nationality led to a hatred and distrust of other races, especially races of another colour. At the end of the nineteenth century there was born a man who spent his life trying to create friendship and trust between the white people of America and Britain and the black races of Africa. His name was James Emman Kwegyir Aggrey, and he was an African from the Gold Coast.

Aggrey was a real African, with a jet-black skin and woolly hair and white teeth, and big expressive eyes, and he was proud of it. He knew and loved the fine qualities of his people, their great strength and power of endurance, their

---

[1] Hsi worked in connection with the China Inland Mission, which does difficult pioneer work in Central China.

[2] These are only a few of the names of such men.

amazing memory and vivid imagination, their loyalty and affection, their capacity to see a joke and laugh with the jolliest, happiest laughter of any people in the world.

When he was eight years old his family became Christians through the Wesleyan Methodist missionaries. He went to their school; at fifteen he was teaching a class of thirty boys in a village twenty miles from his own home, and at twenty-three he was headmaster of a mission school, an accomplished printer, and in training for the ministry. From Africa he went to America, earned his college fees by teaching and proof-reading, took his degrees (M.A. and D.D.), and was ordained in the Methodist Church.

Aggrey was given charge of two negro churches in America, and it was there that he first began to understand and tackle the difficulties of black people. He found his congregations very poor, and feeling that they were despised by their white neighbours. Besides preaching to them he decided to try to help them to help themselves. He got them to raise chickens and sell eggs, and thus they improved their condition, and earned the respect and gratitude of those who lived near them.

But Aggrey's work was not to be limited to this. His love, both for his own people and for

the white men and women who had brought him
the Gospel and his education, his real Christian
faith, and his brains, had been noticed by men in
high position. When the trustees of the Stokes-
Phelps Trust decided to send a Commission to
Africa to enquire into the state of education with
a view to helping it, James Aggrey was asked to
go with them.

Aggrey now had a great chance of helping his
own people, but there were big difficulties to be
faced. In Africa he found white men despising
black, and black men hating white, whilst he
himself was often treated with contempt because
of his black skin, not being allowed to stay in
hotels, or even travel in the same cars as white
people. But he was too keen on his work to
grumble, and too big a man to be hurt by small
insults. When he was snubbed he laughed, and
when men scowled at him he smiled at them.
" Christ's law of non-resistance," he said. He
talked to his audiences in picture language which
they did not easily forget, and when he found
black and white men quarrelling, he said, " You
can play some sort of tune on the white keys of
a piano ; you can play some sort of tune on the
black keys ; but to produce real harmony you
must play both the black and the white keys."
Aggrey travelled many miles in Africa, creating
friendliness and enthusiasm wherever he went.

He wanted the best things for his people. "I plead with the Christian Church to make Africa the first Christian Continent," he said, and he begged for the sort of education that would train Christian character as well as mind, teach people agriculture as well as algebra, and give them all the white man's treasures of learning without destroying the best things in African character and life.

A new enthusiasm concerning education was rising in Africa at this time, and not long after Aggrey set out on his commission the Governor of the Gold Coast decided to establish a college for Africans on these lines. It was to train them from the kindergarten to the university, to be free of Government control, and to be staffed by both black and white men and women who knew the language and customs of the people. Aggrey was asked to become its Assistant Vice-Principal.

Whilst Achimota (as it was called) was being built, Aggrey went about Africa talking about it, and rousing the enthusiasm of his countrymen. In 1927 it was opened. Two thousand people gathered in the great hall, and four thousand stood outside. There were forty African chiefs in their ceremonial robes, labourers, farmers, townsmen, women and children, black and white, African and European stood side by side rejoicing in this new and splendid venture of Christian people.

That year Aggrey died and was mourned in three continents. In America white citizens were his pall-bearers. At Achimota men of many races held a service of remembrance and thanksgiving. In London, at the church of St Martin-in-the-Fields, a West African student sang a dirge for him, commending his soul and his work to God:

" May the Owner of Heaven give him perfect
        peace;
  May his labours immortalise his name;
  May he gain heavenly victory.
  We wish him Godspeed."

NOTES .

CHRIST AND CÆSAR.—Whilst it is true that every race must express the Faith in its own way, it is equally true that a Christian's first loyalty is to his Church, and its claims must stand before those of family or friend or race or nation. The first Apostles suffered persecution for proclaiming that in Christ there is neither Jew nor Greek; the first great company of martyrs died to prove that the kingship of Christ must be put before that of Cæsar. Since that time Christians in every land and age have been ready to give up their lives rather than accept any god or earthly ruler in the place of Jesus Christ, and the story of the martyrs is not ended yet. Within the last hundred years, and now, in our own times, men have been and are sealing their witness with their blood.

CHAPTER XXX

CHRIST OR CÆSAR?

EIGHTEENTH TO TWENTIETH CENTURIES

FRENCH CATHOLICS; GERMAN PROTESTANTS; RUSSIAN ORTHODOX CHURCHMEN

THE early Church respected the State as a community of men who were united to maintain justice (ch. v.), and so long as Christians were not commanded to do wrong, or prevented from peaceably preaching the Gospel, they were urged to obey it.

In the East this obedience to the State (personified by the Emperor) sometimes grew dangerously servile, but in the West, under the strong leadership of the bishops of Rome, the Church maintained its rights. There was a good deal of quarrelling over those rights in later centuries, and this is not at all surprising, for many of the problems they faced have not yet been solved. These problems grew more difficult during the break-up of the Holy Roman Empire and the rise of nations, who wanted to express themselves in their own way and to control the Church within their own borders. The Church did not

246

always understand these aspirations rightly, and sometimes opposed claims which were just; but, on the other hand, those Churches which became associated with national self-expression were always in grave danger of oppression and interference by the State. Churches which were not State-established were in less danger. Nevertheless, all Christians, as members of their nation, may one day have to decide whether they will obey " Christ or Cæsar," knowing that suffering or death will be the result of obeying the Church rather than the State.

This choice came to the early Christians when they were commanded to offer incense to Cæsar as a god; it came to missionaries who were forbidden to preach the Gospel; it came to men and women who were commanded by kings and parliaments to break or evade the rules of the Church.

During the French Revolution such a choice faced the Roman Catholic priests in France. Though many of the clergy agreed with the principles of the new government (civil equality and freedom of conscience), the majority of them went into banishment rather than accept a law which forbade the Pope to institute them, and put them at the mercy of the State. When the State, abolished religion in 1793, the great majority of those who had not been banished or murdered by riotous mobs refused to give up their faith, and bishops and priests went fearlessly to the guillotine. Freedom of worship was restored two years later, but Napoleon tried to get the Church into his power, and imprisoned and ill-treated the Pope. The result was only to bind Catholics together in greater loyalty, and to make Catholic France more religious than before.

In our own times the Church has been persecuted in Mexico, and in China during the rise of national feeling. In Italy, though there is no persecution, an attempt is being made to assert the supreme power of the State in such a way as to interfere with Christian education.

In Germany intense national feeling has led to worse things. There has been an attempt to alter the Protestant [1] Church into something which is not really Christian at all, to make it an institution which exists to worship the spirit of the German people instead of Christ Who is the Master of all peoples. German Protestants, while loyal to their country and eager to see it restored to prosperity and power, have nobly protested against this. Pastors have been silenced and even imprisoned, congregations forbidden to meet, reports altered, papers suppressed, but the protest goes on. The persecution has drawn the

---

[1] The Protestants, being more closely associated with the State, were naturally in graver danger than the Catholics.

Lutherans and the Reformed Churches together, and in 1934, at Barmen, they published a Confession together, declaring that the Christian Church exists to bring Christ's Gospel to all people, and must never be used as a tool to serve the purpose of any one nation or government.

The most serious persecution of our time broke out in Russia at the Revolution, and is directed at all Christians, but especially at the Russian Orthodox Church.

The Orthodox Church has always been closely linked with the State, and in Russia it had become enslaved to the will of rulers who were often wicked and un-Christian. The Czars had tampered with its government, and before the Revolution the choice of bishops had fallen under the influence of the evil monk Rasputin, who had great influence at Court. Some of the Orthodox clergy disliked the rule of the Czars, and were glad when the Revolution came. At first it looked as if things were going to be better. A new patriarch, Tikhon, was elected and appointed to govern with his Synod. Tikhon refused to be drawn into politics, and advised everyone to submit to the Government when it was not contrary to faith and conscience, but he boldly condemned the Government for killing hundreds of innocent people.

The Bolsheviks began to punish Russian priests

for sympathising with counter-Revolutionary ris-
ings, and to put them to death simply for giving
a blessing to these troops as they passed through
the villages. Then they began to persecute
Christians only because they were Christians. In
1918 Churches were deprived of their property,
their wealth, and even of their sacred vessels,
though the full money value of these had
been offered instead. Monasteries were turned
into museums, church-buildings into restaurants,
theatres, and ball-rooms. Christians were forbidden to print their books or to teach religion
in their schools. In 1922 horrible processions
went through the streets of Moscow and other
towns, carrying hideous or foolish figures meant
to represent Our Lord, Christian priests, and the
holy men of other religions. In 1923 the Roman
Catholic Archbishop Cieplak, Monsignor Budkie-
wicz, and many others, were tried and condemned
to imprisonment, banishment, or death. Tikhon
had already been imprisoned, and died in 1925,
no one knows how. An Anti-God Society was
formed to try to root religion out of the hearts
and minds of the Russian people.

From this dark and terrible country have come
tales [1] of the suffering and heroism of the Russian
Christians. We hear of men and women who, in
the midst of all this, manage to get churches open,

[1] These were reported in 1934.

and, half-starved themselves, somehow manage to get enough white flour to make the Holy Bread. We hear of exiles in Siberia practising their religion. There is the tale of an old priest, caught by the Red Guards and asked why he was not afraid of torment and death; he answered, " The power in us is of God: martyrdom is a new rose in Christ's crown." We are told of a transport of Churchmen going into exile carrying lighted candles as at a festival, and singing the ancient hymns of their Church which tell of the power of the Risen Christ over Death and Hell.

Persecution is once more purifying and strengthening the Christian Church. German Christians tell us that they feel a new sense of the power and presence of God. In Paris Russian priests are training themselves so as to be ready to return and help their people. And all over the world Christians of every denomination are drawing nearer to each other in order to proclaim and defend the Faith of the Church.

NOTES   .   .   .   .

THE REUNION OF THE CHURCHES.—We have seen that from very early times there have been divisions in the Christian Church. Sometimes these have been due to misunderstandings created by different languages, race-jealousy, or political troubles, but often they were the result of deep convictions and real disagreement among Christians. Men felt that Our Lord's commands were being disobeyed, His teaching corrupted, His Church dishonoured, and that they must separate from their fellows, suffer, and even fight, rather than let that happen. The separation of Christians within the Church is a horrible thing, yet there were noble ideals and fine heroism behind some of those old quarrels and divisions and persecutions.

The divisions began as early as the second century ; then the Eastern and Western Churches separated, and other groups broke away from the Eastern Church. The Lutheran and Reformed Churches and the English Church became separated from the Roman Church, together with some who kept most of the Catholic beliefs and customs but repudiated the supremacy of the Pope. (These were called *Old Catholics*.) The Lutheran and Reformed Churches divided again ; from the English Church arose the Congregationalists, Baptists, Friends and Methodists, and both Methodists and Presbyterians in Scotland were again subdivided.

During the last century Christian people have become more and more ashamed of their unhappy divisions, and more ready to draw together in

sympathy and understanding. We saw that persecution by pagans has united some, and others
have realised that it is hard to preach the Gospel
of Christ to non-Christians when those who bear
His name cannot worship or work together.
Many men and women to-day are working and
praying for the time when they will be united in
a Holy Catholic and Apostolic Church which is
free, and in which everything good which any
one group of Christians has stood for shall be
kept and shared by all.

This spirit has shown itself in a number of
different ways. *Christians of many denominations
are now working together wherever they find it possible
to do so.* The STUDENT CHRISTIAN MOVEMENT,
which arose among Christian students at the end
of the nineteenth century in England and America,
and is now represented in thirty-five countries, is
working for friendship and understanding and
co-operation among the Churches. In 1906 a
UNITED COUNCIL FOR MISSIONARY EDUCATION
was formed. In 1910 a great WORLD MISSIONARY
CONFERENCE met at Edinburgh, representing all
denominations except the Orthodox and Roman
Churches, and out of this Conference arose an
INTERNATIONAL MISSIONARY COUNCIL. In 1925
there was another inter-denominational Conference
on Life and Work, and in 1928 a World Missionary
Conference was held at Jerusalem in the Summer

Palace lent by the Patriarch of the Orthodox Church there. To this conference many representatives of the newer Churches in Asia and Africa came to tell of their difficulties and of their ideals for the Church of Christ. Fifty-one countries were represented.

There have been conferences to discuss the agreements and differences between the Churches, and the difficulties in the way of reunion. In 1920 the bishops of the English Church met and issued " An Appeal to all Christian People," calling them to repent of their divisions and work for reunion. Many conferences arose out of this, the most important being the one which met at Lausanne in 1927 and represented all Churches except that of Rome. Since 1920 bishops of the English Church and leaders of the Free Churches have frequently met to talk about reunion together.

Some Churches have recognised others as parts of the Catholic Church, and in some cases inter-communion has been established. The Patriarchs of the Orthodox Church are not able to meet together in council at present, but three of them have declared that they believe the English Church to be a true part of the Catholic Church, though not in agreement with themselves on some important things. The English Church and the Old Catholics have established inter-communion (1932), and English bishops have helped to consecrate bishops of the

Church of Sweden, which follows the teaching of Luther on many points.

Churches which had split up into a number of small sections have become one Church again. In 1929 nearly all the Scottish Presbyterians; in 1932 nearly all the Methodists.

Different denominations have united to form one Church. This has happened in Canada among the Congregationalists, Methodists, and most of the Presbyterians; and there is a scheme for uniting the Episcopal and Free Churches in South India.

Although so much has been done, there is a good deal of misunderstanding and prejudice to be overcome, and some real differences of outlook which have not yet been reconciled. No Christian and no Church must give up what is really believed to be the will of Christ for His Church just in order to be friendly.

The deepest differences lie between the Roman Church and the rest. In 1870 the Roman Catholics held a great Council (THE VATICAN COUNCIL) which set forth two dogmas [1] to be believed by all its members, one of which was the infallibility [2] of the Pope. At the end of the century the

---

[1] A dogma is the statement of a truth which need not be discussed because it has already been decided upon.

[2] This does not mean that everything the Pope says is perfect and unalterable : he is only held to be infallible when, as head and spokesman of the Church, he defines a doctrine or moral commandment which is to be held by all its members.

question of English Church Orders was discussed, and Roman theologians decided that they were not valid [1] (1896). This made it very difficult for those who had been trying to see a way of uniting the English Church with the Roman Catholics, but they refused to be discouraged. A fine French Lazarist priest, the ABBÉ PORTAL, and a group of English Churchmen led by LORD HALIFAX, determined to continue the discussions they had been having together. They were be-friended and helped by a great-hearted Belgian Cardinal-Archbishop, DESIRÉ FRANÇOIS JOSEPH MERCIER of Malines.

[1] A word meaning "having no force." The Romans do not believe the English Church to have maintained the Apostolic Succession.

CHAPTER XXXI

THAT THEY MAY BE ONE

NINETEENTH AND TWENTIETH CENTURIES

DESIRÉ FELICIEN FRANÇOIS JOSEPH MERCIER, 1851-1926

DESIRÉ MERCIER was born in the little village of Braine Alleud, near Brussels, where he lived and went to school, earning what he could in playtime by delivering parcels in the village. His father was dead in those days, his mother was poor, and there were four sisters and another brother to feed and clothe. The brother, Leon, became a doctor, but Desiré wanted to be a priest, and when Father Oliviers of Braine Alleud was made vicar of a church in the Cathedral city of Malines, he went with him. There, in the College of St Rombaud and the Seminaries, Desiré began his training, three hours of prayer and nine hours of study on every weekday but one. He was a tall, dark, lanky boy, very high-spirited, and with a tremendous capacity for hard work.

Mercier became a deacon, then an instructor in the Seminary, and then a priest. He went on with his teaching and his studies, and he came to have a great love and reverence for the writings of

St Thomas Aquinas. At this time the Pope was also thinking a great deal on the same subject; he decided to establish a school for the study of St Thomas's works at the University of Louvain, and Mercier was chosen to be its head.

Mercier did not only want his pupils to study St Thomas's writings, but to apply his principles to the learning of the twentieth century. He taught them never to be afraid of new knowledge, but to remember that this is God's universe, and that theology and philosophy and science and art and every aspect of learning are all parts of one great harmony of truth.[1]   To prepare himself for his work he studied psychology under the great scientist Charcot in France, and chemistry and mathematics and biology in Belgium.

In 1906 Mercier was made Archbishop of Belgium, and a great carillon was played on the bells of the city when he entered the Cathedral Church of Malines. There in his palace he lived as simply and strictly, and worked as hard, as he had done when he was a poor scholar. In spite of all his other work he still wrote a great deal, and one of his chief desires was to get his people to love and understand the noble liturgy of the Roman Church, and to worship together with reverence at its daily services.

[1] All Christian thinkers believe this, though not all of them think that St Thomas's way of teaching was the best.

In 1914 the great European War broke out, and the Germans invaded the neutral territory of Belgium. Mercier's country was like a besieged city. Except for the food which was allowed to come in from America, they were cut óff from all other people but the Germans. The Archbishop was allowed to go to Rome to elect the new Pope (for he had been made a Cardinal), and when he got back to Brussels he heard that the University of Louvain was burning, and his cathedral and palace under shell fire. He went back to his shattered city, but it was impossible to stay there ; he went to Antwerp, where the fortifications soon began to be smashed up by German shells, and there he waited and faced the coming of the enemy. Mercier demanded that the religious worship of the country should be allowed to go on ; he got his way, and he went back again to Malines. There he faced all the horrors brought about by an army of occupation, organised relief for hunger and suffering, comforted his people, and by his pastoral letters restrained them from acts of violence and revenge. With superb courage he faced the German Commander, General von Bissing, and protested against cruelty and wrong and outrage of every kind. He would not be silenced, and he answered those who tried to check him in the words great Churchmen have always used in speaking to tyrants : " We must

obey God rather than men." Mercier was a
patriot, and he called every Christian to love his
country, and if need be, to suffer and die for it;
but he was too great a man to hate his enemies,
even the men of the German army. There is a
story which tells how he once found a young
German lieutenant in church, and, learning that
it was his twentieth birthday, took him home to
dinner with him, and gave him a blessing and a
parcel of books and goodies to take back to the
line.

The Great War ended, and there was famine
and sorrow and bitterness and confusion of
thought everywhere. Mercier helped Polish and
Russian exiles, housed Hungarian children in his
diocese, sent relief to the sufferers in Chinese
famines and Japanese earthquakes. His heart went
out to all who were suffering pain or striving
after goodness. He had read the English Archbishops' "Appeal to all Christian People," and
he gladly agreed that the Abbé Portal and Lord
Halifax and their friends should meet in his palace
and talk about the reunion of the Churches. So
in 1921 they came to him, not as official representatives, but as Christians who wanted to face
all the misunderstandings and difficulties and dis-
agreements that lie between the Churches of Rome
and England, and see if any way might be found
to reunite them. Each side was loyal to the

Church it represented, and while some difficulties were cleared away, there were great problems which they could not solve. Yet they were not dismayed. As Mercier said, they could not see how they could be united, yet they knew it must be possible, because Christ wished it, Who had prayed concerning His followers that they might be one. During those "Conversations" at Malines there grew up a fine friendship and mutual respect between the men who sat round the Cardinal's table, and especially between Mercier and Lord Halifax. In one sense nothing was done at Malines: in another sense something very great was accomplished. For the first time since the sixteenth century Roman Catholics, and those who were separated from them, discussed their big differences and the sad, bitter quarrels of their past in friendship and trust and peace.

In 1926 the Cardinal lay dying of an incurable disease in the hospital at Brussels. He called the Abbé Portal from France and Lord Halifax from England; they knelt together in his room at Mass, and then Mercier put his arms round Halifax and laid his head on his heart. From his finger he took a ring, presented to him by his family when he became a bishop, and gave it to him. Lord Halifax wore that ring till he died, and afterwards it was set into a chalice which is used in York Minster to this day. Two days afterwards the Prayers for the Dying were said. The Archbishop made his last effort, giving up his life to God in an act of prayer for the three things he most cared for. ." Offer your life for the Church," his confessor said, and the old man, too weak to speak, bowed his head. " Offer your life for your country and the welfare of your people." Again Mercier bowed. " Offer your life for the reunion of all the Christian Churches." The white head bent this time, not once, but three times. The last few prayers were said, and then came silence. A hospital bell tinkled, and there came a deep solemn clanging from the church tower near by. And afterwards, from all the high carved towers in city after city, the bells of the Belgian churches cried out to the world that a great servant of Christ and His Church had gone gloriously home.

EPILOGUE

CARDINAL MERCIER served the Church of his times as a priest and scholar, just as Kingsley served it as a social worker, Wesley as an evangelist, St Louis as a knight, St Methodius as a translator, Perpetua as a martyr. In every age men and women have so served in some special way as the need was greatest.

We ourselves live in big and dangerous times. There is need of Christian service of many kinds —of priests and scholars, governors and economists, farmers and manual labourers, artists and scientists, doctors and engineers—every profession and craft can express the mind of the Lord of all good life, and contribute something to the community called by His Name. And if our times grow more dark and dangerous, the Church will need martyrs too.

The Christians whose stories have been told here belonged to many different denominations. Yet there is a sense in which we can say that they all belonged to one Church, to the great company of those who call themselves by Christ's name, worship Him as the Son of God, and strive to obey His will.

This book has been written that its readers may love and honour and loyally serve the denomination to which they belong. It has been written that they may love and honour even more deeply the great Church of all the twenty centuries of Christendom, and so live and think and work that all misunderstandings between Christians shall be done away, and that the whole body of Christ's people may go forward with faith and courage to win the world to His obedience.

A SHORT BOOK-LIST
FOR TEACHERS OF CHURCH HISTORY AND OLDER STUDENTS
(Revised 1960)

BOOKS marked A are source-books, contemporary or very early accounts of the happenings in each period. Other books recommended are written by persons who are in sympathy with the character of the denomination with which they deal. It is exceedingly important that the history of every part of the Christian Church should be studied from the point of those who belong to it and understand it from the inside, as well as from general records. Since this list was first compiled time and a major war account for some excellent books being now out of print, but such books (marked *) can generally be obtained in libraries, and County Libraries are especially helpful. Good encyclopædias, e.g. Chambers', are also valuable.

WORLD HISTORY

A. * *Readings in European History*. C. H. Robertson. Ginn.
Ancient Times: A History of the Early World. J. H. Breasted. Ginn.
Cambridge Mediæval and Modern Histories.

CHURCH HISTORY

History of Christianity. K. Latourette. Eyre & Spottiswoode.
The Church of our Fathers. Roland Bainton. Scribner's (Charles) Sons, New York.
Documents of the Christian Church. H. Bettenson. O.U.P.
A History of the Church in England. J. R. H. Moorman. A. & C. Black.

CHAPTER I

A. The New Testament.
A. *Documents Illustrative of the Early History of the Church to
    337 : A New Eusebius.* S.P.C.K.
   Beginning at Jerusalem. J. Foster. Lutterworth Press.
   * *The Conflict of Religions in the Early Roman Empire.*
    T. R. Glover. Methuen.

CHAPTER II

A. *Early Christian Fathers.* Ed. C. C. Richardson. S.C.M.
    Press.
   Documents Illustrative. As above.
   Persecution in the Early Church. H. B. Workman. Epworth
    Press.
   Atlas of the Early Christian World. Nelson.
   The Kingdoms of Christ (many illustrations). P. Bamm.
    Thames & Hudson.

CHAPTER III

A. *Life of St Antony by Athanasius.* Longmans.
A. * *The Lausiac History of Palladius.* W. K. Lowther Clarke.
    (Preface important.) S.P.C.K.
   The Early Church and the World. C. J. Cadoux. T. & T.
    Clark.
   The Saints of Egypt. de L. O'Leary. S.P.C.K.
   The Desert Fathers. H. Waddell. Constable.

CHAPTER IV

A. *Documents Illustrative.* As above.
   Early Christian Doctrines. J. N. D. Kelly. A. & C. Black.

CHAPTER V

Augustine : Confessions and Enchiridion. Ed. A. C. Outler.
    S.C.M. Press (also in Fontana Books, Collins).
Life of St Ambrose. S.P.C.K. (Paper.)
Life of St Augustine. Catholic Truth Society. (Paper.)

CHAPTER VI

A. *The Rule of St Benedict*. J. McCann. Burns & Oates.
   St Benedict : His Life and Work. A. Lindsay. Burns & Oates.
   The Monastic Order in England. D. Knowles. C.U.P.

CHAPTER VII

A. *A History of the English Church and People*. Bede. Penguin Books.
   St Patrick : His Writings and Life. N. D. J. White. S.P.C.K.
   St Columba of Iona. L. Menzies. Iona Community.
   England and the Continent in the Eighth Century. W. Levison. O.U.P.

CHAPTER VIII

A. *Life of Alfred* (Asser). O.U.P.
   Religion and the Rise of Western Culture. C. Dawson. Sheed & Ward.

CHAPTER IX

Lives of SS. Cyrill and Methodius in Baring Gould's *Lives of the Saints*.
The Russians and their Church. Nicolas Zernov. S.P.C.K.
Byzantium. Ed. N. H. Baynes and H. St L. B. Moss. O.U.P.

CHAPTER X

St Bernard of Clairvaux. Watkin Williams. Burns & Oates.
Life of St Bernard in G. G. Coulton's *Five Centuries of Religion*.
Mediæval Europe. H. W. C. Davis.

CHAPTER XI

A. *Selections from the Little Flowers of St Francis.* S.C.M. Press.

A. * *The Lives of the Brethren* (Dominican). P. Conway. Burns & Oates.

St Francis of Assisi. J. R. H. Moorman. S.C.M. Press.

St Dominic, Pilgrim of Light. G. K. Brady. Burns & Oates.

CHAPTER XII

A. De Joinville's *Chronicles of the Crusades.* Dent.

An Atlas of Mediæval History. McEvedy. Penguin Books.

CHAPTER XIII

A. *Nature and Grace : Selections from the Summa Theologica of Thomas Aquinas.* Ed. A. M. Fairweather. S.C.M. Press.

Aquinas. F. Copleston. Penguin Books.

CHAPTER XIV

A. *The Ancren Riwle.* Ed. J. Morton. Burns & Oates.

The English Mediæval Recluse. F. D. S. Darwin. S.P.C.K.

The Legacy of the Middle Ages. Ed. C. G. Crump and E. F. Jacob.

An Outline of European Architecture. N. Pevsner. Penguin Books.

Church Life in England in the Thirteenth Century. J. R. H. Moorman. C.U.P.

CHAPTER XV

A. *In Praise of Folly.* Erasmus. Allen & Unwin.

The Renaissance. E. Sichel.

CHAPTER XVI

A. * *Documents of the Continental Reformation.* B. J. Kidd.
   The History of the Reformation. J. P. Whitney. S.P.C.K.
   Here I Stand: A Life of Martin Luther. R. Bainton.
   Muller.

CHAPTER XVII

* *Documents,* etc. As above.
The Scottish Reformation. G. Donaldson.
Portrait of Calvin. T. H. L. Parker. S.C.M. Press.
Calvin. Emmanuel Stickleberger. James Clarke.

CHAPTER XVIII

St Francis Xavier. J. Brodrick. Burns & Oates.
Apostle of the Indies (Xavier). C. J. Stranks. S.P.C.K.
The Counter Reformation. B. J. Kidd. S.P.C.K.

CHAPTER XIX

A. *The First Prayer Books.* Dent.
   The Story of the Prayer Book. V. Johnstone and E. Evans.
   Mowbray.
   The English Reformation to 1558. T. M. Parker. O.U.P.

CHAPTER XX

A. * *Chronicles of the Pilgrim Fathers.* Dent.
   English Religious Dissent. E. Routley. O.U.P.
   Baptists who made History. A. S. Clement. Carey-
   Kingsgate Press.

CHAPTER XXI

A. *The Journal of George Fox.* Dent.
   The Quakers: Their Story and Message. A. N. Brayshaw.
   Allen & Unwin.

CHAPTER XXII

A. * *Six Saints of the Covenants*. Patrick Walker.
   The Covenanters. J. Beveridge. T. & T. Clark.
   The Scottish Reformation. G. Donaldson. C.U.P.

CHAPTER XXIII

Life of St Vincent de Paul. H. K. Sanders. Heath Cranton.
St Vincent de Paul. C. J. Martindale. (Paper.) C.T.S.

CHAPTER XXIV

A. *Selections from the Journal of John Wesley*. S.C.M. Press.
   Life of John Wesley. John Telford. Epworth Press.
   Hugh Bourne, 1772–1852. J. T. Wilkinson. Epworth
   Press.
   William Clowes, 1780–1851. J. T. Wilkinson. Epworth
   Press.

CHAPTER XXV

A. *Apologia pro Vita Sua*. J. H. Newman. Fontana Books.
   Life of John Mason Neale. G. Towle. Longmans.
   Oxford Apostles. G. Faber. Penguin Books.

CHAPTER XXVI

A. *Carey's Enquiry into the Obligations of Christians to use
   Means for the Conversion of the Heathen*. Carey-Kingsgate
   Press.
   A History of Christian Missions. C. H. Robinson. T. & T.
   Clark.

CHAPTER XXVII

A. *Charles Kingsley, his letters and memories of his life*. By his
   Wife. Macmillan.
   Church and People, 1789–1889. S. C. Carpenter. S.P.C.K.

CHAPTER XXVIII

A. * *In Darkest England.* William Booth. Salvation Army.
   * *God's Soldier.* St J. G. Ervine. Heinemann.
   William Booth. M. L. Carpenter. Salvationist Publishing
   Supplies.

CHAPTER XXIX

Dr Aggrey. W. M. Macartney. S.C.M. Press.
Creative Tension. S. Neill. Edinburgh House Press.

CHAPTER XXX

A. * *The Church Controversy in Germany.* Anders Nygren.
   S.C.M. Press.
   The Russians and their Church. Nicolas Zernov. S.P.C.K.
   The French Revolution. Hilaire Belloc. O.U.P.

CHAPTER XXXI

A. *Documents on Christian Unity.* Ed. G. K. A. Bell. O.U.P.
   The Ecumenical Movement. K. Slack. Edinburgh House
   Press.
   Men of Unity. S. Neill. S.C.M. Press.

INDEX

A

Abelard, 79, 98, 103
Agapé, 9
Aggrey, 238
Aidan, 51, 56
Alban, 17
Albertus Magnus, 100, 102
Albigenses, 89
Alcuin, 59 ff.
Alfred, King, 65-66
Altar, 9, 34, 109, 158
Ambrose, St, 35
America, 152, 165-168, 175-176, 215
Andrew, St, 4
Andrewes, Bishop, 158
Anglo-Catholics, 202 ff.
Anscar, 134
Anselm, St, 82, 100
Antony, St, 20 ff.
Apologists, 18
Apostles, 49
Apostolic Succession, 40, 154, 256
Apse, 8
Aquinas, St Thomas, 24, 100 ff., 258
Arius, 27 ff.
Arminius, 185
Art, Christian, 14, 73, 110
Athanasius, St, 24, 26, 27 ff.
Augustine, St, 24, 27 ff., 35, 38
Augustine, Missionary to England, 51, 53

B

Bacon, Roger, 100
Baptism, 6, 168
Baptists, 168
Barclay, Robert, 176
Barnardo, Dr, 237
Barrowe, Henry, 162
Basil, St, 26, 72
Baxter, Richard, 170, 223
Becket, Thomas à, 82, 113
Bede, The Venerable, 57
Benedict, St, 44 ff.
Benedict Biscop, 56
Bernard of Clairvaux, St, 75 ff.
Bernardine of Siena, St, 125
Bible (Scriptures, Gospels), 7, 9, 25, 62, 69, 131, 118-119, 158-160
Bible Society, 213
Bishops, 8, 40
Blandina, St, 14
Bonaventura, St, 100
Boniface, St, 57-59
Booth, William and Catherine, 230 ff.
Bossuet, 192
Bradford, William, 163, 167
Brendan, St, 56
Bridget, St, 56
Browne, Robert, 162
Bucer, Martin, 134
Bunyan, John, 169
Busher, Leonard, 168
Byzantine Empire, 67 ff.

C

Cædmon, 57, 158
Calvin, 136 ff.
Calvinistic Methodists, 200
Cameron, Richard, 183
Cardinals, 80
Carey, William, 215, 217 ff.
Carlile, Wilson (Church Army), 237
Catacombs, 14
Catherine of Siena, 115
Catholic, 42, 151, 203
Cedd and Chad, SS., 56
Charlemagne, 58 ff.
Chivalry, School of, 90 ff.
Christian Socialists 226, 229
Chrysostom, St, 26
Church Buildings (Architecture, 8, 34, 79, 108, 122–123
Church Councils, 32–33, 41, 76, 149, 255
Cieplak, Archbishop, 250
Clare of Assisi, St, 87
Clement of Alexandria, 18
Clifford, Dr, 229
Coffin, Levi, 201
Colet, John, 119
Colleges and Collegiate Churches, 122
Columbanus, St, 56
Columba, St, 51 ff., 179
Congregationalists, 161, 255
Constantine, Emperor, 17
Convocation, 204
Copec, 229
Corpus Christi, feast of, 104
Covenanters, 178, 181 ff.
Cowper, William, 200
Cranmer, Thomas, 124, 152 ff.
Creeds, 7, 30, 32 ff., 72
Crusades, 76, 78, 94
Curia, 80
Cuthbert, St., 56
Cyprian, St, 15, 19

Cyril of Alexandria, St, 26
Cyrill of Constantinople, 67 ff.

D

Dante, 115
Deacons, 8, 40
Diocese, 40
Dominicans, 89 ff., 100, 149
Donatus, 43
Duns Scotus, 100
Dunstan, 66

E

Eadburga, St, 57
Education, Christian, 7, 25, 48, 55–56, 63, 98, 122, 133, 140, 148, 150
Elizabethan Settlement, 154
Elizabeth of Hungary, St, 106
England, Church of, 152, 176, 254–255
Episcopacy, 161
Erasmus, 116 ff.
Etheldreda, St, 57
Eucharist, 9
Eusebius of Cæsarea, 26, 29
Evangelical Revival, 193 ff.
Evangelists, 48

F

Fasts and Feasts, 10, 11, 211
Felicitas, St, 16
Filioque Clause, 72
Fox, George, 171 ff.
Francis of Assisi, St, 83 ff.
Francis of Sales, St, 192
Free Churches, 161 ff., 255 ff.
Friends, Society of, 171 ff, 210 223
Fry, Elizabeth, 200

G

Gall, St, 57, 63
Germanus, St, 53
Gnosticism, 27
Godric, St, 111
Goodwin, Thomas, 170
Gore, Bishop, 229
Government of Early Church, 8, 40
Gregory, St, 53
Gregory Nazianzen, St, 26
Gregory of Nyssa, 26
Gregory VII, 82
Guthlac, St, 111
Guthrie, James, 182
Guyon, Madam, 192

H

Halifax, Lord, 256 ff.
Headlam, Stewart, 229
Helwys, Thomas, 168
Heretics, 27, 90
Hild, Abbess, 57
Holland, Scott, 229
Homoousion, 30
Hooker, Richard, 158
Hours of Prayer, 50, 111, 155
Howe, John, 170
Hsi, Pastor, 240
Huguenots, 142
Huss, John, 116
Hymns, 5, 9, 38, 63, 103-104, 133, 185, 201, 206-207

I

Ilminsky, 213
Immersion, 6, 168
Independents, 169 ff.
Indulgences, 124 ff.
Inner Light, doctrine of, 172, 176

Inquisition, 143 ff., 208
International Missionary Council, 253
Investitures, 80
Irenæus, St, 19
Irish Monks and Schools, 55 ff.
Isaac, Abbot, 23

J

James, St, 4
James the Deacon, 55
Jesuits, 146, 148, 150, 212, 229
Jewell, Bishop, 158
Jews, 8
John of the Cross, St, 149
Jordon of Saxony, Blessed, 90
Joseph of Arimathea, St, 4
Jude, 4
Juliana of Norwich, 111
Justification by Faith, Doctrine of, 129
Justinian, Emperor, 48, 67
Justin Martyr, 18

K

Kagawa, Toyohiko, 240
Keble, John, 202
Kempis, Thomas à, 115
Kentigern, St, 179
Khama, Chief, 240
Kingsley, Charles, 224 ff.
Knibb, William, 201
Knox, John, 141, 180

L

Las Casas, Bartholomew, 149
Latimer, Hugh, 156
Laud, Archbishop, 177, 203
Law, William, 202
Lazarist Priests, 189, 256

Lazarus, Family of, 4
Lioba, 58
Liturgies, 10, 155, 258
Livingstone, David, 217
Lollards, 115, 179
Lord's Supper, The, 9, 140, 164
Louis of France, St, 92 ff.
Loyola, Ignatius, 145 ff.
Luther, Martin, 126 ff.
Lutherans, 133, 149

M

Macarius of Alexandria, 23
Macarius of Russia, 213
Mahomet, 59
Manichees, 38, 104
Margaret of Scotland, St, 179
Mark, St, 4
Marot, Clement, 184
Marsilius of Padua, 115
Martin, St, 24, 45, 54
Martyn, Henry, 215
Mass, 66, 109, 140, 155
Matthew, St, 4
Maurice, Frederick Denison, 226
Melanchthon, Philip, 134
Melville, Andrew, 180
Mercier, Cardinal, 256 ff.
Methodists, 193, 231, 241, 255
Methodius, St, 67
Missions, Foreign, 211 ff.
Monasteries, 21, 47, 63, 90, 106, 122, 186
Monks, 21
Moravians, 193, 212
More, Sir Thomas, 119, 123
Morrison, Robert, 216 ff.

N

Neale, John Mason, 206
Nestorius, 211

Newman, John Henry, 204-205
Nicea, 28
Nikolai, Father, 215
Ninian, St, 179
Nonconformists (Dissenters), 171
Non-jurors, 185, 203

O

Occam, William of, 100, 115
Old Catholics, 252
Orders, 42
Origen, 19
Orthodox (Greek, Byzantine) Church, 72, 215, 249
Owen, John, 170

P

Pagans, 12
Pantaenus, 25
Pascal, Blaise, 192
Patriarchs, 41, 72
Patrick, St, 51 ff.
Patteson, Coleridge, 214 ff.
Paul, St, 4, 14
Paulinus, St, 54
Peden, Alexander, 183
Pelagius, 39, 53
Penance, 42
Penn, William, 176
Perpetua, St, 12 ff.
Persecution of Christians, 12 ff., 244, 246
Peter, St, 14, 41
Pilgrim Fathers, 166
Polycarp, St, 14
Pope, 53
Portal, Abbe, 256
Prayer Books, English, 154 ff., 160, 177
Predestination, Doctrine of 139, 185

Presbyterianism, 139, 180, 185
Presbyters, 8, 40
Priests, 40
Primitive Methodists, 199
Protestants, 133 ff., 142, 152, 158, 160, 248
Psalms, 184, 203
Purgatory, 125
Puritans, 161, 177
Pusey, Edward, 204

R

Raikes, Robert, 200
Renaissance, 116, 223
Reunion of the Churches, 230, 251 ff.
Ridley, Bishop, 156
Robinson, John, 161 ff.
Roman Catholics, 185, 215, 255
Rutherford, Samuel, 180

S

Sainte Chapelle, 95
Saints, reverence for, 113
Salvation Army, 230 ff.
Scholastica, St, 47
Schoolmen, 99
Scotland, Church of, 179 ff.
Serapion, 34
Shaftesbury, Lord, 230
Simon Stylites, 23
Sisters of Charity, 189 ff.
Smith, John, 201
Smyth, John, 169
Social Reform, 222 ff., 229 ff.
Student Christian Movement, 253
Suger, Abbot, 110
Sundar Singh, 239

T

Taylor, Jeremy, 202
Temperance Work, 237
Teresa of Avila, 149
Tertullian, 17, 19
Theodore of Mopsuestia, 57
Theodore of Tarsus, 57
Theodosius, Emperor, 37
Theodulf of Orleans, 63
Thomas, St, 4
Toleration, Edict of 17
Tractarians, 202 ff.
Transubstantiation, Doctrine of, 112, 135
Truce of God, 76

U

Ulphilas, 211
United Council for Missionary Education, 253
Universities, 98 ff.

V

Venianimoff, 213
Venn, Henry, 200
Vestments and Church Colours, 10, 155, 158, 210
Vincent de Paul, St, 186 ff.
Virgins, Order of, 42
Vladimir of Russia, 71
Vulgate, 150

W

Waldo, Peter, 89
Walker, Patrick, 183
Warnefrid, 61
Watts, Isaac, 201
Wesley, Charles, 192, 201
Wesley, John, 193 ff.

Wesleyan Methodists, 199
Whitefield, George, 194 ff.
Wilfrid of Ripon, St, 57
William of Orange, 143
Williams, John, 216, 220
Wilson, Margaret, 182
Woolman, John, 201
Worship in the Early Church,
    8, 34
Wyclif, 115, 158

X

Xavier, St Francis, 144 ff.
Ximenes, Cardinal, 149

Z

Zwingli, 134

PRINTED BY MORRISON AND GIBB LTD., LONDON AND EDINBURGH

Boc